Creating an EVEN Greater Whole

Leadership is not a solo sport; it's about people and how they engage with one another. True leadership isn't driven by an individual's ego, but by the ability to connect, understand, and inspire others. Emotional Intelligence (EQ) enables leaders to shift their mindset, empowering their teams to reach their highest potential. *Creating an Even Greater Whole: Becoming an Emotionally Intelligent Leader* offers managers a fresh perspective and practical tools to navigate their leadership journey.

"This book is a must read for all managers and business leaders who want to create positive workplace cultures. Susan Schwartz's expert advice combines outcome-tested strategies with practical "know-how" to build and manage strong teams. It is required reading for all those who need to drive high retention and profitability…and satisfy customers anywhere in the world."
—**Susan Kudla Pineno,** *PMP, Adjunct Lecturer, School of Continuing Studies (SCS) Project Management Program, Georgetown University*

"Emotional Intelligence is critical for good, effective, leadership. Susan Schwartz takes the "Theory" of Emotional Intelligence and presents understandable, practical and actionable tools to guide all managers toward a more effective leadership style. *Creating an EVEN Greater Whole* delivers accessible real-life examples and self-reflective prompts which personalize the learning structure."
—**Keley R. Petersen,** *Founder & CEO, Willow Grove Advisors, LLC*

"*Creating an EVEN Greater Whole: Becoming an Emotionally Intelligent Leader* is a thought inspiring book written by a leader in the field of emotional intelligence training. Susan Schwartz turns ideas into actions. She uses examples from history and modern day—including her own experiences—to eloquently elucidate this complex issue. When reading the book, you feel like Susan is talking to you; she creates an emotional environment with safe empathic vulnerability. She literally models her message. Anyone who wants to become a leader or is a leader will be a better leader with Susan's words in their mind and heart."
—**Ashok Bhattacharya,** *MD, FRCP, Founder of the Empathy Clinic*

"Susan invites us to dive into fearless conversations about leadership. This book is the veritable middle ground between theory and practice. Susan's expertise and knowledge reaches its pinnacle in her book where you get to understand and practice your emotionally intelligent skills. This is a must read for anyone who wants to lead effectively."
—**Naïs Mouret,** *Global Leadership Advisor & Emotional Intelligence Consultant*

Creating an EVEN Greater Whole

Becoming an Emotionally Intelligent Leader

Susan G. Schwartz

CRC Press
Taylor & Francis Group
Boca Raton London New York

CRC Press is an imprint of the
Taylor & Francis Group, an **informa** business

Cover: Web Large Image (Public)

First edition published 2025
by CRC Press
2385 Executive Center Drive, Suite 320, Boca Raton, FL 33431

and by CRC Press
4 Park Square, Milton Park, Abingdon, Oxon, OX14 4RN

CRC Press is an imprint of Taylor & Francis Group, LLC

© 2025 Susan G. Schwartz

ISBN: 9781032854755 (hbk)
ISBN: 9781032859705 (pbk)
ISBN: 9781003520719 (ebk)

DOI: 10.1201/9781003520719

Typeset in Minion Pro
by KnowledgeWorks Global Ltd.

To Dave, my true north

and

To my guiding stars:

Emily & Aaron

Carl & Tayler

and

To Miriam, my hope

Contents

Preface

Leadership is not a solo sport. It is about people and how they engage with each other—not the individual leader or their ego. Becoming an Emotionally Intelligent leader is about shifting your mindset for success. As an expert, your performance was measured by how much information you knew. As a leader, you are now measured by how well your team performs.

The transition from "Me" to "We" can be difficult. I've spoken with many people who, when promoted, were afraid they would lose their competitive edge when they shifted their focus to develop the capabilities of their team. This is a normal reaction and it takes time to shift your mindset.

An Emotionally Intelligent leader's ability to focus on core issues, communicate in a powerful way, and neutralize potential conflict seems so easy. **It's not!** It is only through trial, error, and mistakes that leaders hone these skills. People will err. And, for Emotionally Intelligent leaders mistakes are not failures—they are learning opportunities.

As I was making my own journey from subject expert to leader, I didn't understand how people made leadership look so easy. I look back to my "hero" leaders and recognize their Emotionally Intelligent acumen. They were keen observers who asked questions and engaged their teams as active problem solvers. From their example, I discovered leadership depends on continuous learning because the only reality leaders can count on is change. And yes, sometimes people do need to "make it up" as they go along because there is no precedent—the situation truly has not happened before.

My purpose in writing this book is to offer people a different perspective and some tools they can use to more easily navigate their own leadership journey toward becoming an Emotionally Intelligent leader.

Although the content was written with a specific thought flow in mind, it is possible to read the sections in any order. Chapter 1 begins by exploring different traits attributed to leaders. Chapter 2 overviews the practical application of Emotional Intelligence and human-based leadership skills. Continuing forward, Chapters 3 and 4 discuss how to work through the leadership basics of aligning your vision and communicating your message to enable people to understand everyone's roles so they can begin working collaboratively. The conversation is expanded in Chapters 5 and 6 to discuss how to best motivate people so they fully engage and bring their best self into the workplace. Chapter 7 and Chapter 8 explore tools to minimize potentially explosive situations that accompany uncertainty, risk, and conflict. Lastly, Chapter 9 focuses on the human element of leaders and how to use your unique style to navigate the unknown.

Creating an EVEN Greater Whole is a compilation of stories and learnings from my meandering journey. I don't believe this book is an end. I like to think of it as a milestone for reflection and a launch point for future expeditions. There are many people with whom I worked along the way who are too numerous to mention in this small space. To all those who traveled with me, thank you for sharing the journey and helping me navigate across the bumpy moments. Together, we were able to make some good things happen which none of us could have done on our own.

This book is one of those projects that could not have happened without the encouragement, advice, and counsel of trusted friends. Enormous thank yous to Susan Pineno, Lanie Denslow, Ashok Bhattacharya, Keley Petersen, Deb Evans, Frumi Barr, Michaela Cassidy, Jacqueline Wales, and CC Clark for your generosity of time, perspective, and feedback.

Lastly, a thank you to my family who were always there at the end of a long day to remind me what is truly important. My husband, Dave, is my eagle-eyed first round editor. Thank you for always being direct and kind. My children Emily, Carl, son-in-law Aaron, and daughter-in-law Tayler who keep my perspective fresh and up-to-date. I am grateful for your energy and insight. And a special thank you to Emily who after an early read of my first book asked, "What happened to my mother's voice?" The initial drafts were too formal. She reminded me to be authentic and true to the ideas of leadership and honesty I shared with her and her brother growing up. Her advice stays with me and I hope the importance of authentic leadership resonates with you.

About the Author

Susan G. Schwartz is a leadership and management coach who equips expert professionals to become excellent leaders. Based on her experience leading global teams, she takes a practical Emotionally Intelligent approach to build cohesive, collaborative, and happy teams. Her passion fosters inclusive workplaces that encourage people to bring their full human-being to work.

In addition to many years of experience working with corporate, non-profit, and government teams, she holds an M.S. in Organization Development and Knowledge Management. She is an adjunct instructor at UC Berkeley and UC Santa Cruz and a guest lecturer at Georgetown University.

1

Why Is Leadership Important?

> Leaders are defined by...
> Trust enables leaders to...
> Leaders aren't necessarily born...

Leadership is important because people drive business success. For many years, people and culture were left out of strategic conversations which tended to focus on the business triad: process, marketing, and technology. The thread that supports each of the three legs of the success stool is people. Without people, the stool cannot stand.

Emotionally Intelligent leaders know that engaged employees are the driving force behind positive business outcomes, which include higher retention, lower absenteeism, and higher profitability. They assure, by words and actions, employees know that both they and their work are important to the organization.

It is easy to say that effective leaders should build workplace cultures that motivate and engage employees. The question is how. What skills are needed to create and maintain a positive, collaborative work environment? People say they know a strong leader when they see one, but they can't define what makes a leader strong. And, what makes an Emotionally Intelligent leader?

Professional development plans for rising leaders are not made up of checklists. Each person's path to leadership depends on their industry, the type of organization, their past experience, and many other factors. Among all of these differences, there is an essential leadership skill set that

DOI: 10.1201/9781003520719-1

enables them to bring people together to achieve the organization's goals. This book is organized into sections to introduce strategies that enable people to develop leadership skills that will engage employees and realize positive business outcomes. This chapter discusses core leadership competencies. The next chapter introduces Emotional Intelligence and describes how Emotionally Intelligent practices can propel business success. The following chapters introduce leadership strategies that will enable leaders to bring out the best in their employees.

The *Consider and Deliberate* exercises throughout this book were developed to provide you suggested questions that are geared to help you reflect on different leadership concepts and scenarios. Often the best means of honing your leadership skills is to reflect back on your experiences to recognize similar situations and consider the actions you would like to model moving forward and those actions you want to be sure not to repeat. You may insert questions of your own that are more applicable to your specific situation or experience. There is space for you to write your reflective comments, or you may prefer to keep a separate journal.

Your reflection time may be limited to sitting in a traffic jam, waiting in a checkout line at the grocery store, or other situations you might consider time wasting. Just the opposite—these are valuable moments that you can use to reflect on any variety of complexities.

SURPRISE, YOU'RE A LEADER!

Not everyone who takes on leadership responsibilities follows a preestablished career path. Sometimes leaders arise from the most surprising circumstances. A person can be very happy being a member of a team. And "Surprise!!" something unexpected happens and without too much thought they realize a need and step forward to fill the void. They may have minimal experience and may be uncertain of their capabilities, but, Voilà! Suddenly, they are a leader.

Have you ever found yourself suddenly in a leadership position? My first opportunity to lead a project occurred the first time I shadowed an experienced systems analyst for a large telephone system implementation. I was 23 years old and the woman I was shadowing had 10 years of experience. Her pregnancy became difficult, she was placed on bed rest, and suddenly I was in charge. The senior technicians who oversaw the equipment installation were grizzled curmudgeons who looked me up and down and announced their granddaughters were older than me. What could I do? I didn't pretend to be an expert. I worked hard to perform my role as the customer and engineering liaison and asked them many questions. Those two men took pride in their crusty natures. Once I had earned their respect, they were very kind and helpful as we worked together to resolve the problems that always happen during a system implementation. They taught me the value of hard work, humility, integrity, and trust. Of course, the twice-weekly box of doughnuts I bought on my way to the job site may also have helped to build the comradery that evolved into a trusting relationship.

LEADERSHIP: "I KNOW IT WHEN I SEE IT"

Leadership development can be especially difficult for people who are technical experts and spent much of their careers as independent contributors. These high-performing people take up this new role with minimal experience overseeing operational activities or supervising junior staff, and even less training. Yet, they are expected to intuitively know how to build teams, motivate people, manage conflict, negotiate resources, and prioritize risks.

Discovering unexpected knowledge requirements for leaders is a common situation across nearly all fields. A highly skilled physician told me about the learning curve she encountered with the "business" of healthcare activities when she took over as the medical director for the practice. She was expert on human physiology topics but was at a loss when she had to weigh in on staff issues and business decisions. Everyone cannot know everything about everything. I asked her how she was closing her knowledge gap. Her answer was akin to one meeting at a time. Understanding that leadership is built on practice and experience is key. Be kind to yourself; you will make mistakes AND you will learn something from each success and failure.

So how does one learn to be a leader when leadership traits are hard to discern, difficult to measure, and require unfamiliar skill sets? The little-spoken secret regarding leadership success is that most people have leadership potential within them. Some people have easy access to these internal leadership wellsprings and others may need to work a little harder to bring them to the fore. The method for both types of people is the same: observe, reflect, apply, and repeat.

Observation is the key for learning cause and effect. How does someone in a leadership position react to a challenge? If you are fortunate and are able to work under a strong, positive leader, pay attention to how the leader handles a situation and speaks with people involved. If you are working with a difficult manager/leader, you can still take away some very strong lessons. Observe how this leader handles a situation and speaks with people. Then, file away these examples of how you will NOT manage/lead when placed in a similar situation. Reflection is the process of analyzing the positive and negative consequences that can result from the different actions you could pursue before deciding how to handle a challenging situation.

LEADERSHIP BASICS—THE DIAMOND LEADERSHIP MODEL

When people are asked to identify traits that strong leaders possess, they may list 15–20 off the top of their heads. These often include courage, vision, excellent communicator, integrity, honesty, expertise, and charisma. Strong leaders possess many of those skills; however, it is impractical to try to acquire these all at once. If something appears too complicated, people might give up without even trying. Like a golf swing, it is better to focus on honing the fundamental skills before trying to play a challenging course.

The Diamond Leadership Model[1] illustrated in Figure 1.1 identifies five core competencies of extraordinary leadership. Just as every diamond is different with varying levels of cut, clarity, color, and carat, leaders are not stamped from a single standard of excellence. When I've queried people who tell me that they know leadership when they see it, they share anecdotes that represent the intangible facets: trust, confidence, humility, integrity, and empathy.

Trust is an essential leadership attribute that interweaves the other four leadership competencies. At the core, people follow leaders because they trust them to perform with the best interest of the people who work with them at heart. If a leader does not engender trust, the other competencies lose credibility.

FIGURE 1.1
Diamond leadership model.

Of the four primary facets, *humility* is one of the most important, in that true leaders realize everyone, even her-/himself, possesses strengths and weaknesses, which implies an individual cannot usually succeed alone. *Empathy* is the ability of a leader to put him/herself in another's position. Empathetic leaders are able to view a challenging situation from a variety of perspectives and consider the impact an action may have on all associated parties. *Integrity* is defined as performing to expectations in that you follow through with what you have promised to do. The final facet of *confidence* is a matter of competence as opposed to expertise. The leader may be a subject matter expert; however, they know who and how to get things done. When several things go wrong simultaneously, people want their leader to maintain calm and tell them what to do. Even if the leader doesn't have a clue, they will orchestrate everyone on the team to begin the diagnostic and resolution process. The most successful leaders not only appear confident, they also are able to encourage others to become confident.

TRUST

Brené Brown explores the courage that it takes to lead groups within her book *Daring Greatly*. She tells many wonderful stories; however, my favorite metaphor that describes the trust exhibited by a fully functional team is the act of "turning toward each other" as opposed to "turning on each other."[2] Bad things happen. They just do. When trouble happens within dysfunctional teams, the team members pull away from each other and point fingers to apply blame. When functional teams hit a snag, they exercise their trust bond and pull together to work toward a constructive resolution.

Humility, integrity, empathy, and confidence may be difficult characteristics to measure; however, economists and neuroscientists have targeted the impact of trust within work environments as the focus for several research projects. Stephen M.R. Covey recognized a direct relationship between trust and the speed and cost required to accomplish a designated task. This relationship is demonstrated by a simple formula:

TRUST = SPEED / COST

When trust is low within an organization, it takes more time and costs to get things done. When trust is high within an organization, actions are achieved more quickly and at lower cost.

Covey extends his economic driver metaphor to incorporate trust taxes and trust dividends. He levies an 80% trust tax on organizations where trust is nonexistent. These organizations are described as having a toxic culture. People within these organizations actively sabotage other people's efforts, and management focuses on punishing negative activities as opposed to encouraging positive outcomes. As trust improves within an organization, the tax decreases to zero. Covey awards trust dividends to organizations that nurture trust-based environments. He recognizes a world-class trust environment as one that promotes collaborative innovation, transparent communications, employee engagement, and systems alignment.[3] Why would any leader not want to aspire to creating a high-trust organization?

Paul Zak, a neuroeconomist, combines economics, psychology, and neuroscience in order to fully understand how humans make decisions. His research focuses on how neuroscience research can be applied in a business environment to build high-performing, high-trust groups. His findings reflect similar results to those discovered by Covey and his team. He found people who work within high-trust organizations exhibit more energy and are more productive than people who work within lower-trust organizations. Not surprisingly, the people who worked within organizations that maintained a culture of trust reported lower turnover rates and a positive work-life balance. Comparing a broad spectrum of U.S. companies, Zak's team discovered that the average trust metric was 70% out of a possible 100%. The two lowest-scoring elements tracked by the researchers were recognizing excellence and sharing information.[4] The positive take-away is that leaders can improve the trust within their workplaces with minimal effort and budget by using transparent communication techniques and leveraging their innate skills for humility, integrity, empathy, and confidence building.

HUMILITY

Humility is one of the first traits listed when people describe the leaders they most admire. Proverbs and time-honored adages advocate that challenges make leaders stronger, better, courageous, and humble. One of my favorite sayings is, "that which doesn't kill us makes us stronger." However, I have learned some traits we might consider a weakness cannot always be eradicated via hard work; sometimes, we are who we are. And that is why humility is such an important trait for leaders to acknowledge. Leadership is not about perfection. Leadership is about helping other people navigate difficult situations. You need to be honest with yourself and others when you need to reach out to someone else who might have stronger skills in a specific area.

John C. Maxwell, whom the *New York Times* recognizes as a leading expert in the field of leadership, explains humility with a reference from the pastor Rick Warren: "Humility is not denying your strengths. Humility is being honest about your weaknesses."[5] A strong historical example where a leader was able to be successful by being honest about his weaknesses was described by Emmet Murphy in his book *The Genius of Sitting Bull.* He identified *Strategic Humility* as one of Chief Sitting Bull's strongest leadership traits that enabled him to unite the independent Sioux tribes to defeat George Armstrong Custer at Little Big Horn.

In 1868, the U.S. government signed a treaty with the Sioux Nation that guaranteed them ownership of the Black Hills territory. Today, this territory is known as South Dakota; however, this land had belonged to the Sioux Nation for several centuries before the 1868 treaty was signed. Troubles began in 1874 when gold was discovered in the Black Hills. Suddenly, prospectors began to ravage Sioux territory in search of gold. The federal government tried to renegotiate the treaty and offered to purchase the lands. The Sioux tribal chiefs refused to consider any offer.

The tribal lands were not for sale. In 1876, the United States War Department authorized operations to commence against the "hostile" Sioux.

Up until this point, the tribal chiefs of the Sioux Nation were relatively independent governance units and maintained relatively peaceful alliances. In sizing up the strength of General Custer and his troops, Sitting Bull evaluated his strengths and his weaknesses. He also studied the strengths and weaknesses of the other four Sioux tribal chiefs: Crazy Horse, Gall, Four Horns, and Red Cloud. The U.S. troops had many more soldiers and much more firepower than the Sioux possessed; however, Sitting Bull was convinced that, by coordinating their leadership strengths and not fighting separately, they could provide an insurmountable force to defeat Custer and his Bluecoat forces. Chief Crazy Horse brought innovative creativity which fostered brilliant guerilla warfare tactics to the leadership cohort. Chief Gall's contribution was well-organized in-depth planning strategies. Chief Four Horns' contribution was his ability to make connections and build relationships that provided competitive intelligence which could be used against the enemy. Chief Red Cloud, the most senior of the chiefs, brought rational discussion founded on years of experience and factual analysis to ensure all aspects had been considered. Sitting Bull exhibited his unique collaborative skills to build a ring of trust as he convinced the four Sioux chiefs to join together to execute his strategy, enabling each of his potential rivals to head up different groups based on their particular strength without losing control or respect.[6]

Figure 1.2 illustrates how the leadership ring of trust identifies the unique traits of each of these Sioux leaders who possessed multifaceted leadership skills combined to create a holistic strategy. These same skill areas continue to be applied to situations today where people with varying strengths contribute their energies to create a greater whole than they could imagine achieving as individuals.

When trust is present and people are able to relax their guard and share their honest, off-the-cuff thoughts, collaborative brainstorming and networking activities will result, leading to innovative solutions. These solutions have a greater probability of successful execution because the managers involved are able to be honest with each other when analyzing challenges and developing short- and long-term plans.

Leaders need to be aware of their strengths, their motivations, and their priorities, as well as their weaknesses, to understand and motivate other people. The first "Consider & Deliberate" exercise offers you an opportunity to take a moment to reflect on the various elements that comprise your unique personality.

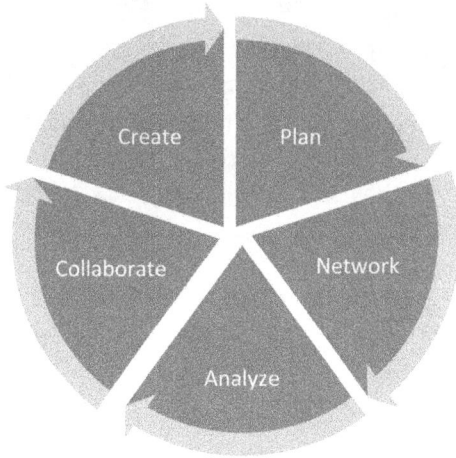

FIGURE 1.2
Leadership ring of trust.

CONSIDER AND DELIBERATE

What three words would you use to describe yourself?

Describe a scenario that illustrates each of the selected descriptive words.

List two areas that you consider weaknesses for yourself. Do you accept each one as part of your organic self? Given the right motivation, what can you do to improve these skill areas?

What skill would your colleagues say you most often contribute to group efforts?

What brings you joy?

How do you channel that joy?

It is relatively easy to recognize the strengths and weaknesses of colleagues and friends. Self-evaluation is never easy. There is no right or wrong answer. This reflection is a tool that you can use to help you understand the personal strengths from which your leadership abilities can develop. The final two questions are important to ask yourself at the end of each day. What brought you joy today? Did you achieve a specific goal? Perhaps you shared in an accomplishment or witnessed a random act of kindness? Did someone impact your day or did you impact someone else's day? Was it as simple as hugging a loved one? How did you share that positive experience with others around you? People who recognize the small moments are that much more astute when it comes to addressing the larger ones.

INTEGRITY

As one of the foundation leadership facets, it is important not to confuse integrity with behaving ethically. Several years ago, I saw a sign in a shop window in Vancouver, Canada, that read, "Al Capone may not have been ethical, but he had integrity." I did a double take. On reflection, I realized Al Capone, who was an infamous gangster during the 1920s, may not have followed the prescribed laws and behavioral mores of the time; however, you could count on him to follow through with any action he promised to dole out. If you welched on a debt and he told you he would break your legs, you knew you had better have some crutches on hand. How many of your colleagues are law-abiding citizens who consistently have excuses why they can't meet deadlines or never follow through on promised commitments? These people certainly are ethical, but they have no integrity since they cannot be counted on to do what they say they will do when they say they will do it.

In addition to following through on commitments, integrity is demonstrated by leaders who perform according to the same rules they set for the people with whom they work. Informally, people recognize a leader's integrity by saying someone walks the talk. They don't make empty speeches demanding people do more with less and then go back to their ivory tower offices with catered lunches. Emmett Murphy describes an example of how not to lead when he describes General George Custer's demand that his soldiers march in full-buttoned uniform carrying heavy ammunition in the hot summer heat. Any deviance from this strict, but pointless, dress code was severely punished. Meanwhile, Custer rode among his troops in a lighter, summer-weight uniform with no equipment and changed to a fresh horse when the one he was riding became tired. He treated his horse with more concern than he showed his reporting troops. In fact, Custer outlined two sets of rules: one he demanded his troops follow and another for himself. In the fury of the battle with Sitting Bull and the Sioux warriors, many soldiers, realizing Custer was safe and well behind the line of battle, broke ranks to save themselves. They felt no loyalty to General Custer because Custer had never shown any care or loyalty for them. [7]

EMPATHY

Some people consider empathy to be a sign of weakness. They believe if you don't demand toughness at all times or if you ask for another opinion, the people reporting to you will consider you weak and not worthy of respect. This is a total misconception. Empathy is not the act of over-sympathizing. Empathy is recognizing how others are impacted by an action. It is about paying attention to the consequences of your decisions. It does not diminish a leader's authority or control.

In fact, empathy is all about paying attention. There is a very powerful line from "The Death of a Salesman" when Willy Loman, who has spent his whole career working for a clothing company, is unceremoniously retired. In his anguish, he screams, "Attention must be paid! Attention must be paid!" He wanted a small piece of respect. He wanted an acknowledgment of his humanity. Empathy is paying attention to the people involved and the impact of the consequences from your decisions—both positive and negative.

When evaluating a new process or procedure, empathetic leaders try to consider how the people who contribute to the process and the people who receive the outputs of the procedure will be impacted by the change. When they reach out to people who can provide a broader view of the problem to help develop the solution, these leaders assure that the solution will incorporate the full organizational perspective to provide a stronger solution than if they had charged forward with a single viewpoint. Strong relationships with long-term allies who stay with you during tough times are another benefit empathetic leaders can reap by practicing inclusion among colleagues and partners.

The preparation for the Battle at Little Big Horn demonstrates the difference between the leadership styles of General Custer and Chief Sitting Bull. Custer didn't believe there was a need to prepare or train the troops following him into battle. Communications and explanations were minimal, if any. His focus was centered on himself and his personal needs.

Sitting Bull, on the other hand, proactively sought out the viewpoints of the various Sioux tribes. The methods he used to motivate them to join together were relatively simple. First, he reached out to establish communications, and then he spoke of his appreciation for the strengths of each party, and then discussed what the commonality the two groups shared.[8] His three-part communication strategy helped him demonstrate his desire to build a relationship and share the goals they could work toward together. Empathy helped Chief Sitting Bull to seek out a broader focus that enabled him to develop a winning leadership strategy.

CONFIDENCE

Some people have a natural swagger, whether they know what they are talking about or not. These charismatic people only talk the talk as opposed to walking the talk. Shakespeare's line from Macbeth, "full of sound and fury, signifying nothing" is an apt description for some people. They will step forward to grab the leadership role; however, they are not able to generate confidence within the people assigned to work with them.

Leaders know how to get things done. They are aware they cannot make everything happen on their own. A confident leader has experience and knowledge that is recognized by the team members, colleagues, and stakeholders to guide everyone's efforts to achieve the designated goal. Their confidence comes from developing an ability to recognize people's talents to create a synchronized effort in which the whole is significantly greater than the sum of the individual parts.

Strong leaders spend much more time asking questions and listening intently than they do telling people what to do. John C. Maxwell sums this concept up when he says, "Any leader who asks the right questions of the right people has the potential to discover great ideas."[9] Confidence happens when people know there are members of their team who can answer the questions for which they don't have the answers. The confidence of knowing that colleagues will support each other during uncertain times is a result of leaders melding the facets of humility, integrity, empathy, and confidence to create the trust necessary to develop and maintain healthy teams.

CONSIDER AND DELIBERATE

For each of the five facets that comprise the Diamond Leadership Model, briefly describe a scenario that reflects a situation in which you were a participant.

Trust:

Humility:

Integrity:

Empathy:

Confidence:

Were your examples all drawn from the same situation?

If not, what similarities do you recognize that are common to each of the scenarios?

For positive scenarios, how can you assure the experience is repeatable?

For negative scenarios, what can you do to assure a positive situation occurs the next time a similar situation occurs?

Different situations will require leaders to draw on different skill sets. In fact, once you become comfortable and have honed one area of leadership expertise, the unexpected will happen and you will need to hone a new set of skills to help your group successfully address a challenge that may never have been addressed before. Focusing on creating and maintaining a culture of trust, even in the most chaotic of situations, will provide an environment that encourages all of your reporting team members, colleagues, and stakeholders to synchronize their best efforts and achieve the goal.

INSTINCTIVE LEADERSHIP

Some people are born with a dominant leadership gene. They are the people who were class president and kickball team captains. Other people are "pegged" as team players. Good team players are hard to find and valued people. However, be careful about putting yourself in a box. It is a great experience for perennial leaders to be a team player once in a while to gain a different perspective and experience a different energy. And sometimes, "Surprise!" great team players will find themselves in a leadership position. Given support, these people often will bring a fresh and energizing perspective to the group. The following two scenarios (one real life and another fictional) describe situations in which an "average Joe" who never considered becoming a leader found he was leading fairly complex work efforts.

JAY COAKLEY AND ELLIE's HATS

Jay Coakley never planned to become a leader. He had spent his career as a middle school gym teacher. He is a humble man who was the kind of gym teacher we all wish we had had. He got bored in retirement and found a position as a part-time elementary school gym teacher. He met a 5-year-old kindergartener named Ellie who was undergoing chemotherapy. She always wore a hat and a big smile. Jay went home and told his wife he would like to give her a hat. They ordered a cute knitted cap from a website. A few of their friends heard about the hat they ordered for Ellie and wanted to contribute more hats. Then, a knitting circle at his church heard about Ellie and wanted to donate hats.

Suddenly, he had more hats than Ellie could possibly wear. He contacted Ellie's mother who helped put him in touch with INOVA Fairfax hospital. His contact suggested the annual winter holiday party would be a good place to distribute the hats. As word continued to spread, knitting circles from as far away as New Jersey and South Africa were sending hats. Requests began to come in from all over the country for hats for pediatric cancer patients. A local restaurant helped him sponsor a fundraiser to pay the shipping costs. Sports teams began donating caps. Jay found himself managing an international team of volunteers. He then received several large checks from people who wanted to help, but didn't knit or crochet. He spoke with his contact at INOVA Fairfax and began a program that provided welcome bags and IPads to pediatric oncology patients. He realized he had done something phenomenal when the non-profit he started, which he named Ellie's Hats, presented the INOVA pediatric oncology program with a $10,000 check.

Jay also helped lobby the Virginia legislature to create a Childhood Cancer Awareness license plate. He received a request from a very ill little boy who wanted his parents to order a pediatric cancer license plate. When his parents discovered there wasn't one, they appealed to Jay. Jay knew nothing of the required process, but he knew people who he thought might know. He called them and asked for their help. Suddenly, Jay was a lobbyist. Jay is quick to attribute his success to the many people who shared their expertise with him when he didn't know how to accomplish a mission task. In only 18 months, Jay Coakley who had never considered becoming a manager became a leader heading up a 501(c)(3) international nonprofit group that now lobbies and raises funds to support children who are fighting cancer. It all started with Jay purchasing a single hat.

LEADERSHIP LESSONS FROM THE LEGO® MOVIE

If you are not familiar with *The Lego Movie*, I'll quickly summarize the plot. The movie takes place in an urban environment ruled by a dictator-like ruler, President Business, and his evil alter-ego, Lord Business. The protagonist, Emmett, is a construction worker who follows the same schedule every day. He is very happy to follow the rules set forth by President Business. A resident wise man prophesied that a "yellow face" who is referred to as "The Special" will rise up to save the world. Emmett is accidentally identified as the prophesized savior. There are several side stories, which include an independent female Master Builder named Wild

Style who creates the most amazing vehicles out of Legos. She introduces Emmett to the other Master Builders who want to overthrow President/ Lord Business. After a false start, Emmett becomes an accidental leader of the team because he can make a plan, follow the plan, and adapt the plan when the team faces a challenge. He works with the Master Builders to deploy the plan that successfully overthrows Lord Business. President Business is "freed" and asks to join Emmett's successful team.

The four primary project leadership lessons I gleaned from the movie that can be used by both new and experienced leaders are:

1. Success is attainable when you believe in your team and yourself.
2. Just because "that is the way we've always done it" doesn't mean that's the only way. People should not be afraid to stand up and suggest an innovative idea.
3. Creative people may be very smart; however, success often requires many skill sets. Subject matter experts need to be able to guide and motivate project teams toward success.
4. A plan that leverages available resources and talent is the essential project foundation.

Plans should not be set in stone. Maintaining a flexible, can-do attitude helps you to evaluate and adapt the original plan to changing situations and keep your focus on the goal.

CONSIDER AND DELIBERATE

How are Jay Coakley and Emmett similar?

Describe a situation when you have watched a single individual (perhaps yourself) address a small need that grew into something larger than you anticipated.

Which of the four project leadership lessons would you select first for your leadership toolkit? Describe a situation where it might have helped to resolve a challenging situation.

What other tool(s) should be included in Emmett's leadership tool kit?

The real-life Jay and fictional Emmett are very practical people. They did not go in search of a spotlight. They began their leadership journeys by proactively seeing a need and looking to how they could close the gap.

They became Emotionally Intelligent leaders because they were able to involve people who had the needed expertise for different tasks. Next, they coordinated the skills and knowledge of the team members to create a whole that could not have been built by the group members had they been working individually. Chapter 2 will explore the attributes that describe specific traits of Emotionally Intelligent leaders.

NOTES

1 © 2017 by Susan Schwartz of the River Birch Group. Reprinted with permission.
2 Brown, Brené. (2012). *Daring Greatly.* (p. 101). New York, NY: Avery.
3 Covey, Stephen M.R. (2006). *The Speed of Trust.* (pp. 13–25). New York, NY: Free Press.
4 Zak, Paul. (January–February 2017). The Neuroscience of Trust. *Harvard Business Review.* pp. 87–90.
5 Maxwell, John C. (2014). *Good Leaders Ask Great Questions.* (p. 33). New York, NY: Center Street.
6 Murphy, Emmett, PhD. (1996). *The Genius of Sitting Bull: 12 Heroic Strategies for Today's Business Leaders.* (pp. 51–88). Englewood Cliffs, NJ: Prentice-Hall, Inc.
7 Murphy, Emmett, PhD. (1996). *The Genius of Sitting Bull: 12 Heroic Strategies for Today's Business Leaders.* (pp. 74–76). Englewood Cliffs, NJ: Prentice-Hall, Inc.

8 Murphy, Emmett, PhD. (1996). *The Genius of Sitting Bull: 12 Heroic Strategies for Today's Business Leaders.* (pp. 76–78). Englewood Cliffs, NJ: Prentice-Hall, Inc.
9 Maxwell, John C. (2014). *Good Leaders Ask Great Questions.* (p. 13). New York, NY: Center Street.

CHAPTER SUMMARY

What Is Leadership?

- Leaders are people who are able to build teams, motivate people, manage conflict, negotiate resources, and prioritize tasks.
- The Diamond Leadership Model identifies the five primary facets of extraordinary leadership: humility, integrity, empathy, confidence, and trust.
- A culture of trust is created by leaders who are able to meld the facets of humility, integrity, empathy, and confidence.
- Humility is the ability to be honest with yourselves and others regarding your strengths and weaknesses.
- Integrity demonstrates a leader's ability to follow through on their commitments.
- Empathy helps a leader recognize how all affected people will be impacted by a decision.
- Confidence is a competency skill that enables leaders to recognize people's talents to create a synchronized effort to achieve a shared goal.

2

Emotional Intelligence and Other Superpowers for Leaders

> Emotional intelligence maximizes ...
> Vulnerability helps leaders...
> Mindless and mindful people view ...

Emotional Intelligence (EI) can be interpreted in a variety of ways. Some people speak about EI as your ability to manage your *feelings* and express them appropriately. I prefer to discuss EI as an action-oriented tool that determines how we choose to behave.

Choice is key to my perspective when I discuss EI because despite how well we might plan, we have no control over other people's behavior. We only can control how we react to a situation. In this way, I prefer to discuss EI as a means to manage your *reactions* to create a positive outcome. Thus, Emotionally Intelligent people "choose" how they will act to create a healthy, inclusive environment that enables people to collaborate and reach shared goals.

A PRACTICAL FIVE-LEVEL MODEL

My practical approach to EI uses a five-element model as illustrated in Figure 2.1. The first, Self-Perception, element speaks to how you perceive your role in a given situation and how well you engage with other people so they recognize your leadership role. You may find yourself in a precarious position when you try to engage with a variety of people who have different expectations for people performing your role. EI enables you to be aware of your behaviors and how they might affect other people.

DOI: 10.1201/9781003520719-2

FIGURE 2.1
Emotional intelligence elements.

The second element targets how you communicate with other people to ensure your message is received as you intended. How can you frame your message so that it is received as you intend for the recipient to hear. This is important because you may need to reframe your message so that people can hear what you mean. For example, you may use slightly different words and tones when you speak with your manager or people who report to you. Messaging awareness becomes extremely important when using e-mail and other electronic platforms because it is very easy for people to misinterpret your intentions. Your words may take on different meanings because they cannot hear your tone.

The third element looks at how well you engage with other people and your ability to create a positive working environment. The fourth element addresses how you handle stress. This includes your skill to recognize how other people handle stressful situations. This strength enables you to guide your team to immediately begin resolving the situation when urgent, timely action is required. The fifth element describes your collaborative strategies and those of the people with whom you are working. Being able to recognize how people prefer to work enables you to create effective collaborative conversations among diverse groups of people.

ENGAGING YOUR EMOTIONAL INTELLIGENCE

On first review, the five-level EI model may be confusing. When someone asks me how they can become a more Emotionally Intelligent leader, I tell them to begin by paying attention. This advice may seem oversimplified; however, paying attention requires intention.

Emotionally Intelligent people follow an intentional four-step action-oriented process:

1. Observe a situation
2. Evaluate the options based on their observations and experience
3. Choose how they will behave to create the positive outcome they desire
4. Collaborate with others who can assist to achieve the goal

---

EMOTIONAL INTELLIGENCE IN THE REAL WORLD

Many studies recognize positive business results when managers practice Emotionally Intelligent behaviors. The president of an IT support firm who attended one of my workshops is an example. A few months after the workshop was completed, he shared this story with me.

Prior to the workshop, he had planned to fire his administrative assistant when he returned to the office because he did not feel she understood the urgency of their clients' problems. One of his takeaways from the workshop was not all people react to stress in the same way. He decided Mary had many fine qualities and he would observe her work for a week before making a decision. He discovered that while he was reacting to a client's call and verbalizing his stress, Mary calmly went back to her desk and began calling people who could resolve the problem. When the president slowed down and observed that not only did Mary understand the client's urgency, she was able to proactively initiate action as well, he realized how valuable Mary was to his company's success. He told me, "instead of firing her, I gave her a raise."

This story is a perfect example of a positive business outcome that occurred because a leader stopped to pay attention, evaluate new information, and choose how they want to act to create a positive outcome. By pausing to observe, the business owner recognized the value of an employee. He told me that if he had dismissed his assistant, he was sure his business would have suffered. He is a better leader today because he tries to understand the workstyles and motivations of his staff. He appreciates the value that people with different workstyles contribute to the company's success.

LEADERSHIP SUPERPOWERS

It would be so simple if we could swallow a leadership pill, fall asleep, and wake up with every leadership superpower at our disposal. Some people will tell you to be careful what you wish for because the outcome might be an unpleasant surprise. For the exercise below, please assume that your wish will only have a positive effect.

CONSIDER AND DELIBERATE

What single leadership superpower do you wish to possess?

Describe how your superpower will help you and your team to address a difficult situation.

Unfortunately, there is no magic leadership pill. Leadership is a skill that needs to be practiced. Even experienced leaders slip up and need to remind themselves to make better choices or behave differently.

The four core leadership superpowers—Vulnerability, Educated Ignorance, Mindfulness, and Emotional Intelligence—are tools that all leaders need to practice. Depending on their role (technical expertise, business management, or strategic leadership), people use these superpowers in slightly different ways. Table 2.1 offers a matrix that overlays the four leadership superpowers and their different roles. The intersection points identify tasks that are performed by the different leadership functions. The rest of this chapter explores the foundation and application of the four leadership superpowers.

TABLE 2.1

Superpower Utilization

Super Powers	Leadership Elements		
	Technical Expertise	Business Management	Strategic Leadership
VULNERABILITY	Risk Management	Change Management	Long-Term Planning
EDUCATED IGNORANCE	Requirements	Scope	Multiple Perspectives
MINDFULNESS	Attune	Acclimate	Adapt
EMOTIONAL INTELLIGENCE	Collaboration	Communication Framing	Engagement and Alignment

VULNERABILITY AND LEADERSHIP

When a crisis occurs, people look toward their leaders to be calm and help guide them through the stress of the situation. All cultures have their version of the British "stiff upper lip" or "keep calm and carry on." When my friends and I were young managers and learning to lead, we were told if we could not mask our emotions, we would be perceived as weak.

Throughout history, leaders are seen as founts of strength and knowledge. I was surprised when I was promoted to a leadership position and realized I didn't have all the answers. It was very difficult to appear confident. I cautiously began seeking advice from people I respected. This is when I learned the greatest secret leaders don't share: they don't have all of the answers—often, they are making it up as they go along. The secret they do share is to gather people who can help you determine a resolution.

In *Daring Greatly*, Brené Brown's explanation of how being vulnerable can transform leadership practices reached out from the pages, grabbed me by my collar, and made me take notice. She discovered the most common fears among C-level executives were not being able to clarify a purpose, remain relevant, and maintain connections. Instead of exposing weakness, her research proved that by recognizing their fears, leaders can use this knowledge as a catalyst to promote creativity, innovation, and learning. Once you've identified the challenge—whether it is lack of information or resources—you are free to imagine what is possible. In fact, the result of refusing to recognize their vulnerabilities will cause leaders and the people on their teams to make excuses, dodge questions, and falsely blame others.[1]

Referencing Table 2.1, organization leaders utilize their vulnerability powers when they analyze risk, address change, and develop long-term plans. It is important to consider what could go wrong to be able to mitigate negative consequences.

CONSIDER AND DELIBERATE

Who was the best manager you ever had? List three traits of this person that made you look forward to returning to work Monday.

How have you modeled these traits to create a positive work environment?

Who was the worst manager you ever had? List three traits of this person which made you dread returning to work every Monday.

Given the wisdom of time and the opportunity for a "redo," how might you behave differently to create a more constructive work environment?

EDUCATED IGNORANCE

I discovered the concept of Educated Ignorance when I listened to Father George Coyne and Brother Guy Consolmagno (former directors of the Vatican observatory) discuss the parallels of faith and science. They explained the parallels that exploration plays in their religious and scientific vocations because each requires them to be seekers in an environment of uncertainty.

It is the awareness of what they don't know—their *Educated Ignorance*—that drives them to continue their spiritual and scientific inquiries. Brother Guy explains his ability to balance science and spirituality with a quote from Anne Lamott, author of *Plan B: Further thoughts on Faith,* "The opposite of faith is not doubt. The opposite of faith is certainty."[2]

Leaders often cannot be certain of an outcome. Educated Ignorance enables us to say it is okay not to have all the answers. It is okay to admit you need more information. It gives you permission to ask questions and explore better answers. However, decisions can't always be delayed until you have all the information you believe you need. Educated Ignorance recognizes, as a leader, there will be situations when you will need to make a decision without full knowledge.

Leaders are empowered and not inhibited by a lack of knowledge. As shown in Table 2.1, Educated Ignorance enables leaders to ask questions, learn about a program/client's requirements, monitor scope growth (or creep), and have the courage to view a challenge through different lenses.

MINDFUL LEADERS

Ellen Langer, a Harvard-based social psychologist, was curious about the traits that differentiated Harvard Business School graduates who succeeded when compared to those who did not perform as well after graduation. She spent a year working on this research project. At the end of the year, she recognized the key traits of mindfulness and mindlessness as a means for determining successful leadership behavior:

Mindlessness is the application of yesterday's business solutions to today's problems.

Mindfulness is the attunement of today's demands to avoid tomorrow's difficulties.

Langer's definitions describing mindless and mindful leadership behaviors provide a new perspective regarding the application of lessons learned.

Just because a strategy proved successful in the past does not mean that it will deliver the exact same results when applied again. The Harvard Business School students who were able to recognize the differences which existed in the current scenario as compared to the original situation were able to mindfully adapt the strategy to serve current requirements and achieve successful results.

The students who applied lessons learned previously without considering shifting circumstances of the current scenario were not as successful as their more mindful peers. Mindless leadership behaviors will not necessarily be labeled as wrong since that the managers and leaders are following organizational traditions. However, those people who can critically assess the situation and adapt solutions to address situational changes will be more effective leaders over the long run.[3]

The phrases, "we've always done it ...." or "the last time, we did ..." are examples of mindless leadership. Mindful leaders address challenging situations from an open frame of curiosity. Referencing Table 2.1, great strength, empowerment, and creativity are exerted when leaders evaluate a situation with consideration of how it was previously handled, what is different today, and what can be done to create success today.

Leaders' awareness about what they don't know enables them to reflect on previous experiences and adapt lessons learned to the current challenge in order to be ready to resolve uncertainties. When I find myself in a difficult position, I like to ruminate on a quote attributed to Marcel Proust: "The real voyage of discovery consists not in seeking new landscapes, but in having new eyes." Leadership is not necessarily about previous performance; it is about having the courage to seek out new solutions that are best-suited to evolving environments.

CONSIDER AND DELIBERATE

What is your greatest fear(s) related to your role as a leader/manager?

What can you do to alleviate this fear(s) or mitigate possible consequences?

When you are asked a question for which you have no answer, what is your initial response?

Do you behave differently if the question is asked by:

Your boss?
Your colleague?
Your reporting staff?
Your friend?

Reflect back on a complex work situation for which the efforts of many people integrated to produce the end product or service. Did you understand the processes that occurred prior to and after your work tasks? What were the reactions of people when you asked questions regarding their work tasks?

Describe a professional/personal effort that required you to adapt your original action plan because of a change in the environment or requirements.

EMOTIONAL INTELLIGENCE AND LEADERS

There is a Chinese parable in which a man goes to a spiritual teacher to discuss how to be happier in his marriage. The wise one listened to the man's complaints and told him, "You must learn to listen to your wife." The man took the advice to heart and returned after a month to say he had learned to listen to every word his wife said. He explained their relationship was improving, but he thought it could be better. The wise one smiled and told him, "Now go home and listen to every word she isn't saying."

Emotionally Intelligent leaders follow the wise one's advice by paying attention to what is said and what is not said, as well as who is speaking and who is not speaking. They observe a situation and choose how they will react to create the constructive outcome they want to happen. For example, when meeting with a client or colleague, do you focus on what you need to accomplish during the meeting or what your client/colleague wants out of the meeting? Essentially, EI is a set of action-based tools that equip leaders to effectively engage their working teams while navigating a variety of situations and relationships.

Referencing Table 2.1, EI offers a powerful framework that describes how people handle themselves and their relationships. It influences how leaders work with collaborative groups, the accuracy of their communications, and their ability to create an inclusive workplace culture.

Workplace cultures are defined by the axiom, "What gets measured gets rewarded and what gets rewarded gets done." Flipping this axiom, an intangible skill that cannot be measured will not get rewarded. How often have you seen a badly behaving "leader" receive kudos and rewards for achieving an easily measured business metric? When this happens younger, rising leaders receive the message that numbers are the only metric that counts. They learn the conversations that discuss employee development and other human-based leadership responsibilities will not improve their bonus. And, they will behave as badly as their current leadership role models.

It is possible to reverse this cycle with tools that can measure leadership traits that previously were not measurable. The next sections of this chapter discuss some assessment tools that measure the intangible capabilities that expand the powers of Vulnerability, Educated Ignorance, Mindfulness, and Emotional Intelligence.

EMOTIONAL INTELLIGENCE AND BUSINESS PERFORMANCE IMPROVEMENT

> Emotions are not feelings at all, but a set of body-rooted survival mechanisms that have evolved to turn us away from danger and propel us forward to things that may have benefit.[4]

(Rita Carter, a science writer and broadcaster)

EI can be defined as the effective engagement of communication and decision-making skills to create a positive outcome. In addition to the Pew and MHS studies, Daniel Goleman, Ph.D., and Reuven Bar-On, Ph.D., pursued extensive research focused on essential leadership skills across a range of industries. The common thread revealed within the documentation from 50+ years of research is the impact non-cognitive (Emotional Intelligence) capabilities have on individual and organizational success.

Daniel Goleman and his team demonstrated the value an Emotionally Intelligent workforce brings to an organization. One of their research projects studied the profit and growth trends of 19 insurance companies. Across all companies, sales agents who scored strongly for emotional competencies such as empathy, self-confidence, and initiative sold premiums that were more than 100% higher than those sold by other sales agents. The high-performing sales agents sold premiums that averaged $114,000, while agents with lower emotional competency levels sold premiums that averaged $54,000.[5]

Current research (2023) validates Goleman's earlier findings. The Gallup organization identified the Gallup $Q^{12®}$ which describes 12 key outcomes that recognize a manager's ability to engage and retain employees. Gallup followed the progress of firms that initiated employee engagement programs by comparing the before and after $Q^{12°}$ data and the associated impact these programs had on absenteeism, retention, and profitability. After one year, the employee engagement programs implemented by the companies that were part of Gallup's research experienced:

- decreased absenteeism (-41%)
- increased retention (+22%)
- increased profits (+12%)

Programs designed around the principles of Emotional Intelligence encourage mutual respect, effective communications, and employee initiative create positive workplaces that will attract and retain top talent.

EQ-I® 2.0 MODEL—A PRACTICAL APPROACH
FOR EMOTIONAL INTELLIGENCE

Reuven Bar-On based his initial human performance research on the question, "Why do some people do well in life while others do not, irrespective of how cognitively intelligent they are?" The resulting EQ-i® 2.0 model that identifies 15 human performance attributes answered this question.

Bar-On's EQ-i® 2.0 human performance formula was developed over a period of 17 years using a rigorous psychometric approach that is used by behavioral scientists to identify and measure human behaviors. The scientific rigor required by the research process assures the results are consistent, free from bias, and addresses a multi-cultural, global workforce. The EQ-i model is the culmination of this research and was the first EI measure to be peer reviewed and commercially available. With this knowledge. Emotionally Intelligent leaders are able to develop mutually supportive relationships with people who can help to achieve the desired goal.[6]

The current EQ-i® 2.0 model identifies 15 human performance factors that are sorted into five categories: Self-Perception, Self-Expression, Interpersonal, Stress Management, and Decision-Making. The human performance factors that comprise Bar-On's EQ-i® 2.0 model are listed in Table 2.2.

People ask if a person can have too much EI or too little. The answer: there is no optimal amount of Emotional Intelligence. The power behind the Emotional Intelligence model is the dynamic engagement of the interconnections between the five primary composites and the associated 15 sub-composites that I refer to as performance factors.

The EI measurement is a reflection of a person's overall abilities at a given point in time. During periods of personal upheaval, someone may not maintain the same level of engagement in certain areas as they may have in the past, or again, in the future. Have you worked with someone who was going through a personal crisis such as an ill child or parent? Did you notice a difference in how they handled a typical situation while their priorities were divided?

The EQ-i® 2.0 is a leadership behavior model that offers a framework for professional development. Even without completing the assessment, you can explore and practice the associated leadership skills.

TABLE 2.2

EQ-i® 2.0 Model

EQ-i 2.0	Composite	Sub-Composite
	Self-Perception	Self-Regard Self-Awareness Self-Actualization
	Self-Expression	Emotional Expression Assertiveness Independence
	Interpersonal	Interpersonal Relationships Empathy Social Responsibility
	Stress Management	Flexibility Stress Tolerance Optimism
	Decision Making	Problem Solving Reality Testing Impulse Control

The rest of this chapter reviews information contained within an EQ-i® 2.0 feedback report that evaluates each of the 15 leadership performance factors. The EQ-i® 2.0 feedback report conveys an individual's engagement for each of the performance factors based on a normal distribution scale (bell curve) illustrated by Figure 2.2. The average population response is represented by the peak of the bell curve which is defined as the mean score '100'. A performance factor score of 100 (the mean) recognizes that a person performs the designated behavior at a level that is higher than 50% of the population and 50% of the population performs at a higher level than they do.

The raw scores (55–145) along the x-axis of the diagram do not correlate to specific linear values of traditional academic grading curves. The scores reflect the relative relationship of an individual behavior as compared with a larger population group. An '87' score does not mean that a person is performing at a 'B' level. Individually the '87' score represents a medium-high performance level for a single data point.

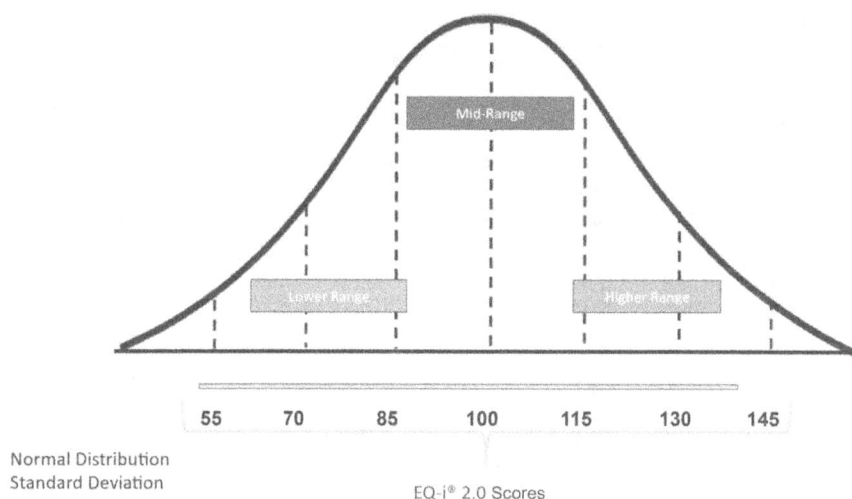

FIGURE 2.2
Normal distribution curve.

When interpreting the EQ-i® 2.0 results, it is important to remember that the 15 different performance factors work in tandem with each other. A score in the lower range does not necessarily identify poor performance just as a score in the high range does not guarantee success. It is a matter of balance between the different performance factor scores.

A person's EQ-i results are a strong predictor of their performance success. Figure 2.3 illustrates a sample snapshot of a top-performing architect. Keiko's EQ-i ® 2.0 assessment results were reviewed and interpreted through the dual context of an architect as well as a leader. Her most well-developed performance factor is Impulse Control. Her least developed factor is Flexibility. As an architect, she can't make rash decisions or deviate even slightly from established building standards. If she makes a mistake, a major disaster could happen because the building was structurally unsound. Her architectural expertise is based on her ability to be precise.

Flipping the lens to interpret her leadership style, the performance factors that made her an expert architect hinder her ability to build relationships and work with people who communicate differently than she does. Keiko's Emotional Self-Awareness performance factor identifies the clarity with which she perceives her expectations for herself and others. The lesser score for the Emotional Expression performance factor limits her ability to express these expectations or initiate difficult conversations with the teams who report to her.

Multiple Role Skills Comparison

Keiko, architect/leader

ES - Emotional Self-Awareness
EE - Emotional Expression
F - Flexibility
IC - Impulse Control

| 55 | 70 | 85 | 100 | 115 | 130 | 145 |

less-developed qualities   *more-developed qualities*

EQ-i 2.0 Scores

FIGURE 2.3
EQ-i® 2.0 performance predictor scenario.

Based on her well-developed Impulse Control performance factor, she did not always communicate in a timely manner because of her desire to choose her words carefully. This leads to a negative cycle where, while Keiko is trying to find the right words to communicate her message, her team continues working without her counsel and the outcome does not meet her expectations. Keiko then becomes angry, criticizes the team, and often takes the work to do herself so it can be done "right." The team is demoralized.

Although Keiko has the best of intentions, she does not recognize the team's need for her to clarify her expectations and provide interim check-ins to help them stay on track. Her rigidity regarding building codes and standards that make her a successful architect does not help her provide appropriate support and counsel for the project teams who report to her. Her lesser engaged Flexibility score hinders her effectiveness as a leader.

Keiko was not a bad person, she did not know how to be a manager. The performance factors were not innate to who she was. Working with a coach, Keiko discussed specific workplace situations and explored alternative methods she could use to better communicate with her staff. Keiko acquired skills to frame her message so that it was received (heard) as it was intended.

The EQ-i® 2.0 assessment results are not meant to be judgmental or used to categorize people. The EQ-i framework is a means to recognize a whole person—their strengths and areas that may not be as engaged. When looking at EI as a balance of behaviors, it is possible to identify position types that will best use a person's unique performance factors and enable them to succeed.

CONSIDER AND DELIBERATE

Of the 15 sub-composites identified in Table 2.2, which four do you think are strengths for you?

Of the 15 sub-composites, which two do you consider weaknesses for you?

Can you describe a situation when your identified strengths balanced out your identified weaknesses?

There is a reason one of the recurring themes of this book is the importance of recognizing your weaknesses as well as your strengths. What one person considers a weakness may actually be a strength. A single performance factor does not drive a leader's success. It is the amalgamation of all performance factors that shapes a person's leadership style.

EMOTIONAL INTELLIGENCE AND
LEADERSHIP PRACTICES

When people engage human-focused Emotionally Intelligent practices, immediate positive workplace results will be realized. This section discusses several real-life examples where intentional actions improved business processes, culture, and profitability.

The following scenario illustrates how the EQ-i ® 2.0 assessment results can be used by colleagues to develop strategies to create stronger relationships. Annette, a start-up restaurant owner, and Tom, the head chef and business partner, have worked together for several years. When restaurant operations are running smoothly, they have a strong business partner relationship. When a stressful situation occurs such as a pipe bursting, a key employee quitting, or the freezer breaking, their strong working relationship suddenly disappears. Since stressful situations are a regular occurrence in the restaurant, this friction needed to be addressed.

Figure 2.4 provides a comparison of Annette and Tom's EQ-i˚ 2.0 assessment results. The lighter squares represent Annette's most and least developed performance factors. The darker squares represent Tom's most and

FIGURE 2.4
EQ-i® 2.0 workstyle comparison scenario.

least developed performance factors. The polarity of each of their strongest skills and weakest skills summarizes their communication conflict story.

Annette's Emotional Self-Awareness and Emotional Expression performance factors reflect her strong communication abilities. She has relatively low levels for the Stress Tolerance and Problem Solving performance factors. When something happens to cause her stress, she will freeze. She cannot solve a problem until she has been able to talk through different options with someone. On the other hand, Tom is a problem solver and jumps into action to fix whatever needs fixing. He is not a strong communicator and does not see the need to discuss different solutions since he prefers to figure out how to fix it on his own. In fact, he began to physically avoid Annette when she wanted to discuss a problem. Both are frustrated and feel the other is totally unreasonable.

When we met to discuss the EQ-i® 2.0 assessment results and their communication difficulties, they began to understand the source of their friction. We discussed how they could adapt their workstyles to be a more effective team. One strategy they discussed was training Annette to use the restaurant trouble-tracking system that Tom and his assistant, Carlos, used to monitor the resolution of smaller and bigger problems. They also agreed on a priority-level system to determine when an immediate conversation was needed and identified an alternate staff member who could assist with less urgent situations. These new strategies enabled Tom and Annette to minimize the conflict that was a result of their different problem-solving workstyles and allowed them to focus on expanding their business.

WORKPLACE BEHAVIORS

A person's EI is defined by the relationships of different performance factors that influence their behavior. Table 2.3 explores a sampling of behaviors that might be observed at various engagement levels. The purpose of this table is for you to better understand yourself and team members.[7] I caution leaders from thinking linearly and sorting people into well-defined categories. This information is meant to be used to help you better understand your and others reactions to develop stronger relationships and develop your leadership style to best guide your employees to become collaborative team members.

TABLE 2.3

EQ-i® 2.0 Engagement Performance Elements

EQi-2.0 Performance Factor	Engagement Level	Practical Observations
Self-Perception Emotional Self-Awareness		Self-Focus and understanding of your relationship with others
	Medium-High	Respond logically based on trigger recognition and understanding of potential outcomes
	Extreme High	Self-indulgent and makes decisions without regard to the situation reality
	Low	Often feel misunderstood and surprised by actions of others
Self-Expression Independence		Confident communications and ability to discuss different viewpoints
	Medium-High	Comfortable contributing to conversations and will discuss opinions
	Extreme High	Authoritarian viewpoint and prefers not to participate in group conversations
	Low	Indecisive and depends on others to make decisions for them
Interpersonal Social Responsibility		Focus on group well-being and building trustful, cooperative relationships
	Medium-High	Focus on collective group well-being with attention to motivation, feedback, and recognition
	Extreme High	Selfless and prioritizes others' needs to the detriment of their performance and well-being
	Low	Disrespectful and insensitive to group needs
Stress Management Flexibility		Ability to adapt thoughts and behaviors
	Medium-High	Confident addressing change and adapts appropriately
	Extreme High	Easily bored and unable to stick to a plan
	Low	Lack curiosity and rigid in their resistance to change
Decision-Making Problem Solving		Recognize impact emotions on solution solving
	Medium-High	Logically addresses problem and coordinates the solution-solving team
	Extreme High	Knows the solution to every problem
	Low	Conflict avoidant and uncomfortable during difficult situations

Using the Self-Perception performance element as an example, you might observe an employee (Lee) become very quiet during a team meeting when someone strongly disagrees with them. You might shrug and think Lee is not a strong team player because of their reaction when their suggestion was not chosen. Or, you might ask to speak with Lee after the meeting to better understand why they stopped talking. During your conversation, Lee shares their frustration because the rest of the team ignored their idea and they no longer feel valued. Lee's perceived personality problem has become a professional development opportunity. How can you help Lee learn how to better communicate ideas with other team members?

The low engagement level for the problem-solving performance factor is another interesting example to review. Many of your team members will approach a problem using a logical approach and encourage others to join in the brainstorming discussion. There are times when someone will not participate or be frustrated that other people don't see an obvious solution. Often, it is wise to step back and observe the situation. If their behavior begins to be a problem for members of the group, you may want to check-in with them to discover why they are disengaging from the collaborative process.

When someone on your team avoids conflict and difficult conversations, invite them to have a conversation with you. You may discover that they may be worried that they don't have the needed technical knowledge, they might be introverted, or a number of other reasons. It is a leader's responsibility to create a working environment where everyone can participate.

You may want to individually approach people who need more time to process information or feel nervous around boisterous colleagues ahead of a group meeting. This side conversation enables them to prepare, enabling them to confidently participate in the meeting. You can also use this side meeting to ask probing questions that recognize their competencies and validate their ideas. If they still don't participate in collaborative discussions, you have the opportunity to gently prompt them during the meeting to share their ideas.

On the other hand, almost every group has a person who knows the solution to every problem. For these people, it is important to nudge them along to consider other possibilities by asking probing questions and encouraging others to participate to launch a productive solution solving conversation.

CONSIDER AND DELIBERATE

Does anyone you know currently, or in the past, exhibit any of the extreme high behaviors described in Table 2.3? Does this designation help to explain their behaviors? With this knowledge will you treat them any differently?

If you find yourself on a new project in which the other team members seem to misunderstand your suggestions, what might you do to gain understanding and acceptance?

What might you say to one of your team members who always seems surprised by their colleagues' reactions to their suggestions?

Describe a recent situation in which you did not express yourself as effectively as you would have liked. What circumstances prevented you from communicating the information you wanted to share.

How might you facilitate a group conversation with people who don't want to participate in an open discussion because they either are convinced their answer is the only solution or simply want other people to make decisions without their input?

Describe a demanding or unexpected situation that arose as part of your personal life and the perceived consequences. What were your initial thoughts and physical sensations? As you worked through the stressful situation, how did your thinking and physical sensations adjust?

How does your ability to manage stress differ between work and home?

There are no simple answers for Emotionally Intelligent leaders to successfully navigate difficult situations. During this reflection did you find yourself also considering aspects of the other attributes of Vulnerability, Educated Ignorance, and Mindfulness discussed within this chapter? These four leadership superpowers combine with one another to provide a strong foundation to manage uncertainty and transform traditional thinking into newfound strengths and innovation.

The EQ-i ® 2.0 Emotional Intelligence model is a framework that provides guidelines to better understand Emotionally Intelligent behaviors. It is not necessary to complete an assessment in order to take your first steps to bringing Emotional Intelligence into your workplace. It is simply a matter of paying attention to the situation and your reactions. The key is how you choose to react.

Emotional Intelligence and the associated performance factors provide a framework to help you recognize your workstyle and consider how you can engage with other people who work and think differently than you. These skills enable you to bring out the best in people as they model your efforts to adapt their behaviors to solve problems and support change efforts. For example, engaging with Educated Ignorance will encourage team members to become part of the solution-solving process and take ownership for its successful execution.

As you start to intentionally bring Emotionally Intelligent actions into the workplace, it is important to:

1. Focus on the behaviors you observe
2. Evaluate the situation from a variety of perspectives
3. Choose how you will act to achieve the outcome you desire
4. Collaborate with others who can assist you to complete your goal

Future chapters discuss Emotionally Intelligent techniques that improve employee engagement and the resulting positive business results that include increased retention, decreased absenteeism, and increased profitability.

NOTES

1 Brown, Brené. (2012). Daring Greatly. (p. 15; p. 207). New York, NY: Gotham Books.
2 Tippett, Krista. On Being. (August 8, 2016). "The Universe Participates in the Mystery of God."
3 Tippett, Krista. On Being. (September 10, 2015). "Science of Mindlessness and Mindfulness."
4 Kaku, Michio. (2014). The Future of the Mind. (p. 34). New York, New York: Doubleday.
5 *Goleman, Daniel. An EI-Based Theory of Performance.* {Chapter 3; The Emotionally Intelligent Workplace Cary Cherniss and Daniel Goleman. 2001; pp. 27–44} *Retrieved from Consortium for Research on Emotional Intelligence in Organizations* (www.eiconsortium.org)

6 Bar-On, Reuven. What it means to be emotionally and socially intelligent according to the Bar-On model. Retrieved February 14, 2017, from http://www.reuven-baron.org/wp/43-2/

7 Stein, Steven and Book, Howard. (2011). The EQ Edge—Emotional Intelligence and Your Success. Jossey-Bass.

CHAPTER SUMMARY

Emotional Intelligence and Other Superpowers for Leaders

- Emotional Intelligence provides an opportunity for people to manage their reactions so they can make decisions that will assure the outcome they want to achieve.
- By recognizing fears and vulnerability, leaders can use this knowledge as a catalyst to promote creativity, innovation, and learning.
- Leaders are empowered and not inhibited by lack of knowledge. Educated Ignorance offers a leader the opportunity to explore new methods and ideas.
- Mindfulness is the attunement of today's demands to avoid tomorrow's difficulties. Just because a strategy proved successful in the past does not mean it will deliver the exact same results when applied again.
- Successful business executives design performance review programs around the principles of Emotional Intelligence to encourage mutual respect, effective communications, and employee initiative to create positive workplaces that will attract and retain top talent.

3

Aligning Teams and Steering the Journey

Leaders align action and vision by…
Boundaries help leaders focus…
Setting priorities enables leaders to…

LEADERSHIP REQUIRES MORE THAN A TITLE

Being an Emotionally Intelligent leader means you are accountable for the actions of the people around you. It means you need to figure out how to motivate your team or organizational group to come together to deliver goods and services complying with scope, budget, and schedule. It means you need to continually pay attention and align the actions of every person who is part of the team.

Managing and leading groups of people is incredibly hard work. Whether your role is that of a supervisor, a manager, an executive, or a strong team player, functional leadership does not mean you get to order people around. Essentially, "in charge" means being where the proverbial buck stops. The leader is the hardest working person of the team. Cartoons showing executives with their feet up on their desk while everyone else scurries around does not represent reality.

Keeping teams focused and aligned is difficult during normal operating circumstances. When situations occur that are outside of your team's control, the immediate tasks can seem nearly impossible. As people's stress levels rise, their attentions may diverge as they begin to look to escape from the situation at hand. It becomes the leader's primary responsibility

DOI: 10.1201/9781003520719-3

to calm their team's worries and help them maintain their focus and energies on what and why of the task at hand.

And sometimes, a leader needs to let people with expertise take the lead during a difficult situation. Chris Hadfield, the first Canadian astronaut, learned that being the Commander of the International Space Station did not mean that he was qualified to make every decision. He describes a leadership lesson he learned during one of the first NASA training exercises for the space station crew. His team was dropped on top of a mesa with minimal gear. He immediately began giving orders, and no one was in front of him to listen. They were already organizing themselves. The other team members had participated in similar exercises and had knowledge and experience that Hatfield did not have. When he got over his initial frustration, he saw that the other team members were collaboratively working out how to work their way down. He discovered that having a title did not mean he automatically knew the "best way" to do something. He learned that leadership means leading the way and not hectoring other people to do it your way. In fact, a strong leader knows when to "get out of the way." He learned that leading his peers required a different skill set. In his previous managerial roles, he was the expert and told people what needed to be done. He realized that he needed to learn when to guide people through difficult situation and when he needed to let them guide.[1]

MANAGING AND LEADING

What does it take for managers and leaders to be successful? Is every manager a leader? What skills make a good manager? What additional skills are required by a strong leader?

A widely accepted lens identifies a manager as someone who assures the tasks required to achieve a goal are completed as smoothly and quickly as possible. Another way to describe a manager role is that a good manager keeps the wheels of defined possibilities oiled and working smoothly while leaders find people with the right skills to make what seems like an improbable scenario possible.

Just as a good manager may not make a great leader, some excellent leaders do not make very good managers. Reflect back on people you've observed to be excellent managers and those who you consider to be strong leaders. What skills or traits would you try to model?

CONSIDER AND DELIBERATE

What makes a strong manager?

What makes a strong leader?

Name four people who you consider to be great leaders.

List management and leadership skills you feel you need to develop for your professional development. Identify the top two skills in each category you would like to prioritize to include in your professional development plan.

There is no right or wrong answer to this reflection. When I facilitate this exercise during a class, people often list manager traits that involve technical expertise, budgeting skills, resource management, clear communications, and respectful behaviors. The management skill sets and knowledge requirements vary from class to class based on the industry and experience level of the course participants.

When the workshop participants were asked to list great leaders and the reasons why they selected these people, many people had a difficult time naming specific non-tangible leadership skills; however, they were able to share instances (or stories) about the leaders they identified. The leadership skills described by their stories were consistent across all classes and mapped to the five skills that were defined as part of the Diamond Leadership Model in Chapter 1. The traits they shared included the ability to:

- admit when they didn't know an answer (humility)
- do what they say and say what they mean (integrity)
- view a situation from someone else's perspective (empathy)
- instill confidence and convince people they have what it takes to achieve a difficult challenge (confidence)
- have their back (trust)

The key takeaway for me from these discussions is that leadership is about people. Technology, tools, and procedures will change, but people's desire for respect, appreciation, and accomplishment never goes out of style.

GROUND ZERO FOR LEADERS

Ralph Waldo Emerson is credited with the phrase, "Life is a journey, not a destination." Extending Mr. Emerson's metaphor, leadership is a meandering journey that starts at a leader's personal ground zero. Just as you and your team become comfortable on a path toward your goal, some type of change will occur and you will need to determine an alternate means to get there. An Emotionally Intelligent leader needs to be confident of his/her starting point or "ground zero" and have a fairly good idea of how they relate to the mission's end goal. Some people call this point a person's "true north." When challenges or environmental shifts alter the initially planned roadmap, the leader's primary responsibility is to make sure their actions and those of the group continue to align and contribute to the end goal.

Once you are aware of your "ground zero" point and have an idea of your immediate path, you can begin to help the people working with you to find their ground zero. The following reflective exercise is designed to help you tackle one of the toughest challenges for a leader, which is creating a plan for yourself.

CONSIDER AND DELIBERATE

Describe your professional/personal status today.

Describe where you want to be professionally/personally a year from now.

What is your plan to reach your destination(s)?

No matter how complex and multifaceted an organization grows, strong leaders are aware of the direction for their own journeys. They set time aside for professional development and are open to new learning opportunities.

Although major changes may not entail the same type of life and death circumstances faced by astronauts, there are times when the need to pivot the trajectory of your current journey can seem like a crisis for you and everyone involved. Change is scary—even if you are one of the people initiating the change. Leaders need to acknowledge the challenge, mitigate as many concerns as they can, and focus the teams on where they need to go.

During June 2013, Colonel Scott A. Jackson learned he would take command of the 3rd Infantry Division's 2nd Armored Brigade Combat Team which had just been designated as one of 10 army brigades to be downsized as part of the budget reduction mandated by the Budget Control Act of 2011. The U.S. military had not gone through this type of exercise in many years—certainly not in the memory of these soldiers. The Spartans, as this unit was known, returned from a tour in Afghanistan to learn the Brigade was to be "downsized" and assumed this meant they were being "fired" from the army. Jackson knew he needed a plan that addressed the basic concerns of the 3,800 soldiers who reported to him, which included the following: Did they have a job and if so would their working units be transferred intact or separated?

The low morale of the Spartan Brigade and the families in attendance at the Change of Command ceremony was evident as Colonel Jackson stepped forward to accept the responsibility of the brigade command. He began his command acceptance speech by addressing the core concerns of his new team and their families: "The first thing that's most important for you to know is that you and your families are going to be taken care of. Nobody gets fired in the Army, so every one of you who chooses to stay in the Army will have a home." He assured the soldiers that most of them would stay within their units and be absorbed into the other 3rd Infantry Division's brigade.

Once he had assured the soldiers that their basic needs would be addressed, Colonel Jackson finished his speech by telling them that their immediate mission was to train as hard as they could to maintain and improve their readiness so that when they were transferred from his command, they would be reporting to their new assignments as the best-trained soldiers in the U.S. Army. His acceptance of command speech ended with the Spartan team shouting the Spartan motto, "Send Me," at the top of their voices to demonstrate their commitment to achieve the mission their Colonel outlined.

In less than three minutes, Colonel Jackson reenergized the brigade, confirmed their value to the Army, and aligned their focus toward the immediate actions which will help them get to the next step of their journey.

Colonel Jackson then began the intense work of developing a plan that would assure a smooth personnel transfer and the divestment of 52,000 pieces of equipment. He infused this mission with the energy that he pursued in every other mission, demonstrating his five core personal values:

(1) people matter, (2) we only succeed when we work as a team, (3) maintain discipline which means approaching routine tasks with a common and high standard, (4) integrity—do the right thing because it is the right thing to do, and (5) balance your multiple priorities of work, health, and family.

He led by example and used continuous communications as his primary leadership tool to help the Brigade maintain focus over the next 17 months. He provided his team information as he received it. When the decommissioning date was set, Jackson began to carry index cards with each soldier's name and assignment as it was set. Any soldier could stop the Colonel to ask after an assignment. If the soldier voiced a concern that Jackson couldn't answer, he made a commitment to find the answer.

When Colonel Jackson officially deactivated the 2nd Brigade on January 19, 2015, 68% of the team had been absorbed into the other Brigades at Fort Stewart, Georgia. The working units (approx. 2,580) people remained intact. Most of the rest of the brigade retired or made a career transfer. A very small number of people (2–4%) were required to transfer outside the original unit because they held highly specialized skill sets which could not be used at Fort Stewart.

The entire process happened over the course of 17 months. The smooth transition can be attributed to the nine months of precise planning that preceded the eight-month deactivation process. The overall goal which stayed constant was to maintain a state of readiness and atmosphere of trust among the cohort of soldiers.

Colonel Jackson attributed the smooth and successful transition to the strategic vision provided by the ability of his senior officers to manage changing priorities and the expert execution performed by the junior officers. He viewed his Brigade Commander Role as that of the chief communicator who assured everyone has the information they needed to perform at their best.[2]

ALIGNING COMMUNITIES FOR SUCCESS

Once you have identified your ground zero, the next step is to learn about the people who will be traveling with you on your journey. I use the phrase "stakeholder" to describe anyone associated with a program, project, or task. Individual stakeholders work together as a community of people who will help each other achieve the designated goal. It is the combined efforts of all stakeholders that will enable a successful completion. If each stakeholder only focuses on their individual responsibilities without regard to how their roles and responsibilities impact other people, the outcome is guaranteed to be filled with conflict and errors.

Some people use the term "village" or "tribe" to describe the interrelationship of people and roles. Whether people reference a community, village, or tribe, the constructive energies developed from these groups engender the trust and confidence that will achieve the shared goal. Nadia Bolz-Weber, a 21st-century theologian, describes this concept best when she said, "I don't think faith is given in sufficient quantity to individuals necessarily. I think it's given in sufficient quantity to the community." Leaders need to make sure that the people who they are leading understand the ground zero for the group and that each individual realizes their own personal ground zero within the organization community and how their role(s) interconnect with the other community members.

Simon Sinek describes the protection people receive when they are part of a coordinated community as the Circle of Safety. He attributes the comradery that develops among tightly connected people as the power that enables collaborative problem solving. Each person is so attuned to their interlocking activities that when one notices something is awry they signal everyone that there is a problem to merge their resources to resolve the issue. If an outside danger such as someone intent on undermining leadership's efforts tries to enter the Circle of Safety, aligned groups will shrug off the negative endeavor. When groups are not aligned and only pay attention to their specific tasks, the danger may not be recognized until the damage incurred is past the point of repair.[3]

When the unexpected happens, people look toward leaders to maintain focus and keep people on track. In the midst of uncertainty and doubt, leaders are the ones who maintain calm and keep people focused toward the designated goal. They prioritize the important factors and redirect energies that are being wasted on trivial matters.

Who were the people in your life, other than your parents, whose actions or words made you feel confident in the face of uncertainty? They might have been a coach, a teacher, a community leader, a manager, or a client. Reflect back on wise words they shared with you that you still repeat to yourself today. How do you model those behaviors? As a counterpoint, for a very brief moment, reflect back on those actions that you found so abhorrent that you promised you would never repeat them when you were in a leadership position. How do you prevent yourself from modeling poor behaviors?

CONSIDER AND DELIBERATE

In your career, has someone stood out as a very strong leader, or a very weak leader? List their names in the space below.

Briefly describe an instance of positive or poor leadership behavior.

In hindsight, what about the positive leadership examples did you find reassuring? What was missing from the poor leadership behaviors?

Describe a situation in which you demonstrated strong leadership skills based on lessons you took from one of the above examples.

A common denominator among strong leadership examples is the leader's ability to encourage behaviors that will help the group to focus on a common purpose or mission. Weaker leader examples often describe someone who does not take responsibility for decisions, blames others, or stirs up conflict among group members. Great leaders understand that group success is really about a community of people who come together to make something happen. A leader's primary role is to assure that everyone's individual effort aligns with the organizational mission and purpose.

ALIGNMENT AND LEADERSHIP GPS

Just as GPS systems help drivers navigate unfamiliar routes, leaders provide a similar function to align and integrate the efforts of their teams as they navigate unfamiliar territory. When people are spread across distances and organizations, it is easy for them to get sidetracked and adjust priorities. The leader's role is to maintain steady communications and to know at what time they should intervene to let people know when and why they need to "make a legal U-turn."

Dr. Henry Cloud discusses the importance of leaders being able to set boundaries. He defines boundaries as "what you create and what you allow."[4] Boundaries become tools which allow leaders to say "No" so they can focus on the current priorities.

As managers, many of us believe we have to say "Yes" to all but the most outlandish requests. We just work longer and harder to complete what needs to be done. As you transition to leadership functions, your workload only gets more complex. It is a matter of survival that before agreeing to a request, you take note of how the request aligns with the mission designated for you and your team. Boundaries will help you hone your neural GPS-like functions so that you can focus your efforts on three basic leadership tasks[5]:

- Pay attention to what is important
- Inhibit what isn't important
- Keep team current and on track

ALIGNING TEAMS

The first step toward integrating the efforts of a group or team is for a leader to establish a common purpose and assure that each person knows how they fit into the total effort. I refer to this step as the "why are we here?" and "why do we care?" phase. By aligning each person's efforts with the overall mission, it is much easier for everyone to realize what is important and ignore what is not in order to stay on course. If this process is skipped over, the leader will spend many wasted hours "recalculating the route" to get the group back on track.

Simon Sinek uses the construct of a Golden Circle, in his book *Start With Why—How Great Leaders Inspire Everyone to Take Action*, to describe how leaders can provide a balanced effort of motivation and execution techniques by identifying the "Why, How, and What" of actions and decisions. Figure 3.1 illustrates Sinek's Golden Circle theory. "Why" is located at the inner core of the Golden Circle and offers people clarity of vision in order for them to understand the purpose and background information that drives the designated action. The outer circle designates the "What" which is the desired outcome or product. "How" is the middle circle that connects the "Why" and "What" layers of Sinek's Golden Circle. This layer describes the methods and disciplines needed to take the concept from a vision to reality.[6]

Have you ever been given a task that didn't make sense or was not part of a normal procedure? When you questioned the rationale or correctness of

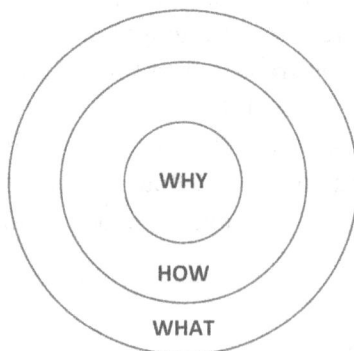

FIGURE 3.1
Sinek's golden circle.

the direction you heard, the person issuing the command told you it was not your job to ask why. How well did you perform that task? Developing strong communication skills and avoiding these types of situations is the basis for Sinek's concept of the Golden Circle and the balance between "What" and "Why." People need to understand how they fit within the greater vision of the organization. No, it is not necessary to share the dressing down you might have received from your boss because things are delayed for no fault of yours. But, what is the story? Why is the task at hand important? Once people grasp the vision, the "How" layer provides the standards, guidelines, and procedures that are used to create the final work product.

Leaders must be confident that people have the skills, understanding, and motivation to perform the tasks and activities required to achieve the shared mission. If any of these are missing, it is the leader's responsibility to close the gaps. If skill sets are missing, they arrange for training or coaching support to assure the people on the team achieve the necessary competency.

When people don't understand their role in achieving the end goal, take a hard look at your communication techniques and the information that you share. If motivation is lacking, initiate a discussion with the affected parties. The solution may be very simple, or it might be a symptom of a deep-rooted problem. Do not let these nagging issues fester among your team members. The situation will only explode at a most inopportune moment.

THE ORGANIZATIONAL CLARITY MODEL

The Organizational Clarity Model[7] illustrated in Figure 3.2 is based on the premise that organizations are made up of different entities that may or may not overlap. The cone represents the enterprise-wide "umbrella." The various entity spheres combine to create multiple aspects of the organization.

The expanded sphere within the second cone highlights the three leadership tiers or layers that exist within each of the organizational entities. The inner tier focuses on the priorities for the leader of the group. The second tier addresses the priorities of the people who are within the leader's immediate working group. The third tier encompasses the strategic priorities shared by

Organizational Clarity Model

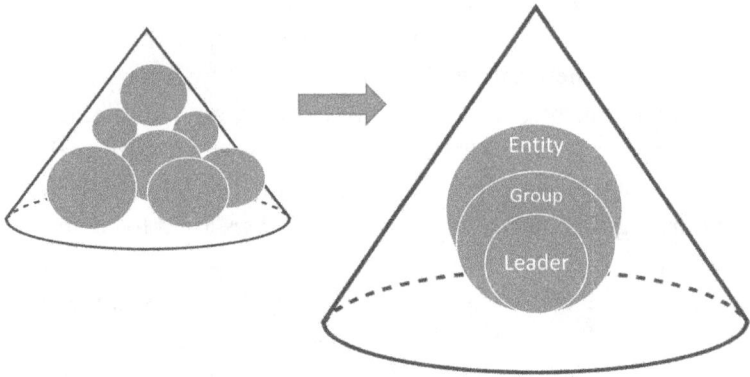

FIGURE 3.2
The organizational clarity model.

all of the groups that comprise the organizational entity. The graphic can be adapted as organizational layers increase or decrease.

The basic priorities of each tier that the leader needs to consider when aligning the vision and purpose for the group are outlined in Figure 3.3. The inner tier traits focus on how a leader views his/her internal self and how he/she reacts to the external views proffered by working group members.

FIGURE 3.3
Aligning group vision and purpose.

The middle tier identifies how a leader defines the roles of people within their department. A leader's success at this level is demonstrated by how they leverage the various strengths and skill sets of the immediate working team to develop a shared group identity and share each other's strengths.

At the outer tier, success is defined by how multiple leaders work together to integrate objectives and align the priorities of the groups assembled within the larger organization. This level of the model is where the group's role within the organization is defined as it integrates with the overall mission.

CONSIDER AND DELIBERATE

Select an organization you work within as a part of your professional or personal life.

Place yourself at the inner core and sketch the organizational structure using the Organizational Clarity Model.

Briefly identify the mission and purpose of each of the three tiers.

How do the three tiers align?

If there are multiple entities within the high-level organization (the cone), how do the various missions of the entities align with that of the primary umbrella organization?

Leaders must constantly think at a variety of levels incorporating potential consequences. What appears to be a simple situation can become very complicated as people from multiple entities begin to work together. Essentially, a leader becomes an organizational GPS system able to identify obstacles and quickly reroute the original plan to achieve the designated goal as expeditiously as possible.

LEADERSHIP AND DELEGATION

It is possible for managers to be successful working as individuals. Leaders, on the other hand, cannot achieve their missions by themselves. They must be able to delegate and coordinate the efforts of multiple groups of people to achieve their vision. It truly takes a collaborative village. The strength and energy gleaned from the entire group's knowledge and capabilities is an Emotionally Intelligent leader's superpower that invigorates teams to achieve what can appear to be unachievable.

Some people find it difficult to delegate. Either they feel there is not enough staff to perform the task, or they believe they can do it faster themselves. If you are overwhelmed by your workload, it is important to list the tasks and prioritize those which are time sensitive or time intensive. Then, discuss your priorities with your manager to determine if they are correct. They also may know of other people who can assist you with a few of the tasks.

If you find it difficult to delegate because no one can do it as quickly or as well as you can, it is important to communicate your expectations to the people who need to do the work. Often people deliver poor quality work because no one has told them exactly what information is needed, the desired format for the deliverable documents, and when you want to receive the information.

Several of my clients who were top technical performers did not understand why people did not provide the same quality work that they expected. When I asked if they had outlined their expectations—they hadn't. They learned that they received high-quality results by taking a few moments to communicate the purpose of the task, the available resources, a template for the gathered information, and the milestone delivery dates. It also is important to check in with the people performing the work to clarify any questions or possible misunderstandings.

Within a collaborative village, Emotionally Intelligent people will take on a variety of roles depending on the needs of the situation: sometimes leading, sometimes following, and sometimes working alone as an independent contributor. Being able to leverage other people's strengths independent of your role will increase the power of the effort being extended.

The reflective exercise below asks you to reflect on a few of your successful past experiences comparing your independent work efforts with those that were performed in conjunction with a group of people.

CONSIDER AND DELIBERATE

Think about a recent project or activity:

List tasks you performed alone.

List tasks you performed as part of a group.

How did these two types of tasks differ?

How would you describe your efforts with regard to the two different types of tasks?

What skills did you use working as a group that you did not need when working alone?

Working with people toward a common goal can be energizing or incredibly frustrating. Did you prefer working on the individual tasks or did you prefer the group-based efforts? When you think back to your experiences working with groups of people, which end of the spectrum did you find yourself? If you had an energizing experience, did everyone understand their role and how the various work efforts connected together? If you had a frustrating experience, was everyone working in different directions?

GIVERS AND TAKERS

Often strong leaders are described as people who always take the time to stop and listen no matter how busy they might be. They are described as being generous and open to suggestions. In his book *Give and Take*, Adam Grant describes why helping others can drive a person's success. Grant expands on the basic concept of networking and project stakeholder relationships by dividing people into three categories: Takers, Matchers, and

Givers. Takers are described as people who rarely recognize the needs of others. Matchers specifically pay attention to "quid pro quo" (I'll do this for you and you'll do this for me). Givers are described as people who are more concerned about helping others without regard to themselves.

Each of these three categories of people is able to use their strengths to be successful leaders within different environments. Takers have proven to gain the most positive results when the results are based on a finite win-or-lose outcome. Givers are considered to be stronger leaders when they work with longer term, complex situations. Some explain the basis for these strengths as the Takers' ability to focus on the essential needs of the moment, while Givers hone their talents to build relationships and establish long-term trust among people.

Based on the presumption that Givers by their nature prefer to help others, no one anticipated the results of Grant's research illustrated by Figure 3.4. The top-performing people were consistently identified as Givers. At the opposite extreme, the lowest performing people also were identified as Givers. Takers and Matchers were ranked within the middle of the performance bands. What is the difference among various Givers that would cause such a significant performance gap? Grant's research identified the differentiating factor that so widely separates Givers between the top and lower performance categories as the amount of self-interest a person holds for their personal achievement illustrated by Figure 3.4. The lower performing Givers are *Selfless* individuals who care so deeply about helping others succeed that they place minimal importance on their

FIGURE 3.4
People focus priority performance results.

individual performance outcomes. The higher performing Givers, identified as *Otherish*, enjoy helping other people achieve success and are able to maintain a balance that allows them to achieve their individual performance goals.

Leaders who are Otherish Givers value the time they share with their team members and associated stakeholders because they recognize this time as an investment. The relationships they build participating in giving activities provide them future value above and beyond the immediate act of giving. Moreover, they appreciate that listening to other people's perspectives is both a means to expand their viewpoint and a way to show respect for the individual's contributions toward the team goal.[8]

This chapter described the roles and practices Emotionally Intelligent leaders use to bring people together and create strong working teams. It also discussed the value a thoughtful "No" brings to the workplace. It is a leadership tool that can redirect people's attention from unimportant distractions to focus on what is important. From a different perspective, a leader's ability to say "no, I cannot speak now, I can …" sets a healthy boundary for the leader to complete a task and be fully attentive during the future conversation.

The next chapter will explore different strategies Emotionally Intelligent leaders can use to create responsible collaborative cultures.

NOTES

1 Hadfield, Chris. (2015). *An Astronauts Guide to Life on Earth*. Pan Books: London. Pp. 105–106. (Original Work Published simultaneously in 2013 by Random House: Toronto, Canada and Little Brown: New York, NY.)
2 Colonel Scott A. Jackson (personal interview, May 26, 2017).
3 Sinek, Simon. (2014). *Leaders Eat Last*. (p. 20). New York, NY: Penguin.
4 Cloud, Henry. (2013). *Boundaries for Leaders*. (p. 14). New York, NY: Harper Business.
5 Cloud, Henry. (2013). *Boundaries for Leaders*. (p. 29). New York, NY: Harper Business.
6 Sinek, Simon. (2009). *Start with Why*. (pp. 65–67) New York, NY: Penguin Books.
7 ©2017 by Susan Schwartz of the River Birch Group. Reprinted with permission.
8 Grant, Adam. (2013). *Give and Take: Why Helping Others Drive Our Success*. (pp. 6–158). New York, NY: Penguin Books.

CHAPTER SUMMARY

Leadership and Community Alignment

- Group success happens when people come together with the purpose of attaining a shared goal.
- Strong leaders help people recognize their roles, relate to each other, and integrate efforts.
- The primary role of a group leader is to identify what is important, minimize what is not, and keep people on track.
- Leaders cannot achieve their missions by themselves; they must be able to delegate and coordinate the efforts of multiple groups of people to achieve the target at hand.

4

The Power of Collaboration and Conversation

Groups get things done by...
Collaborative communities are...
Conversation is powerful when...

COMING TOGETHER FOR STRENGTH

The ability to create a collaborative environment is an essential skill set for Emotionally Intelligent leaders. The ability to encourage conversations among team members that enables them to recognize each other's strengths utilizes the four Emotionally Intelligent action principles: observe, evaluate, choose, and collaborate.

I grew up enjoying Charles Schultz's comic strip, *Peanuts*. Charlie Brown and Snoopy were the main characters; however, as the fourth of five children, I particularly related to Linus who was bossy Lucy's younger brother. One storyline that has stayed with me had Linus asking why he should do what his sister told him to do. Lucy told him, "There are five reasons." She then counted her fingers and curled them into a fist. Linus immediately fell into line and did what she wanted him to do. Bullying aside, the concept of a fist is a great metaphor for individuals coming together to be something stronger than they can be individually. Individually, we are like the fingers on a hand. We have unique fingerprints and flexibility; however, when the fingers merge into a unified mass, a more powerful entity is created.

DOI: 10.1201/9781003520719-4

The title of this book, *Creating an EVEN Greater Whole*, was inspired by Aristotle's adage "the whole is greater than the sum of its parts," which describes the synergy that happens when various entities (or people) merge to create positive energies. Strong leaders help collaborative teams identify their unique capabilities and integrate the efforts of all the participants into a unified force to achieve the shared vision.

Whether you are working on a neighborhood event or complex global project, the foundation for collaborative success is determined by how people value each other's contributions. A positive outcome is contingent on the respect each group member has for everyone's contributions. Often the reason a project fails is because group members don't respect each other and so, there is no foundation on which to build trust. They spend more energy looking over their shoulders or erecting silos than they would if they had taken time to learn about the other members and the strengths they bring to the team.

Adam Grant discusses the complexities of developing organizations, which encourage creativity and innovative thinking in his book *Originals.* His research identified skills, potential, and cultural fit as the three most important factors that organizations consider when hiring. In fact, many of the participating organizations identified cultural fit as the most important element they considered when making hiring decisions.[1] Grant cautions leaders who are trying to build innovative organizations to not hire on cultural fit because they may find themselves in a situation of groupthink since many of their new hires will bring similar thinking into the organization. Instead, he recommends that leaders who are trying to build cultures of originality should focus hiring decisions on the cultural contribution a job candidate will bring to the organization. Search criteria should consider what traits and skill sets are needed to broaden the perspective and decision-making diversity of their group.[2]

Collaborative working groups pool the best of everyone's abilities to create something much bigger than could be created by people working alone. A single superstar cannot generate the same level of innovation and value as a group of individuals working together. The power of collaboration is the process used to resolve a challenge. While good things happen when people collaborate, leaders must be cognizant of the investment of time and effort. When there is a time urgency, leaders may not be able to defer to a collaborative process. However, when time and knowledgeable people are available, the diversity of viewpoints will ensure a strong decision.

CONSIDER AND DELIBERATE

Describe a time when you had to resolve a difficult situation by yourself.

What was your first thought?

What was the outcome? How was it achieved?

Describe a time when you had to resolve a difficult situation as part of a group.

What was your first thought?

What was the reaction of the group?

What was the outcome? How was it achieved?

What different types of accomplishment do you associate with each of these situations?

Solving difficult situations as part of a collaborative group usually is easier than working through a problem alone. Yes, there can be conflict and extended discussions; however, what seems to some as "time wasters" are often a prelude to innovative solutions.

CULTURE OF RESPONSIBILITY

A success metric for an Emotionally Intelligent change leader is how well newly merged teams (organizations) develop and adapt to an evolving culture of responsibility. When people come together as a group to develop a solution, there will be discussions about expectations, responsibilities, and rights as illustrated in Figure 4.1. Experienced managers are adept at defining scope and requirements that define expectations. Responsibility and task assignments ensure that work will be completed as expected, while formal and informal norms define workers' rights and performance guidelines that enable a positive workplace culture to develop.

BUILDING A RESPONSIBLE COMMUNITY

Jonathan Sacks writes about the culture of responsibility in his book *The Home We Build Together: Recreating Society*. He began writing the book as a reaction to the global events post-9/11. At that time, he was the Chief Rabbi of the United Hebrew Congregants of Britain and had seen much of the forward-moving, multicultural strides Britain had made begin to erode. He was concerned by what he saw as societal breakdowns and asked

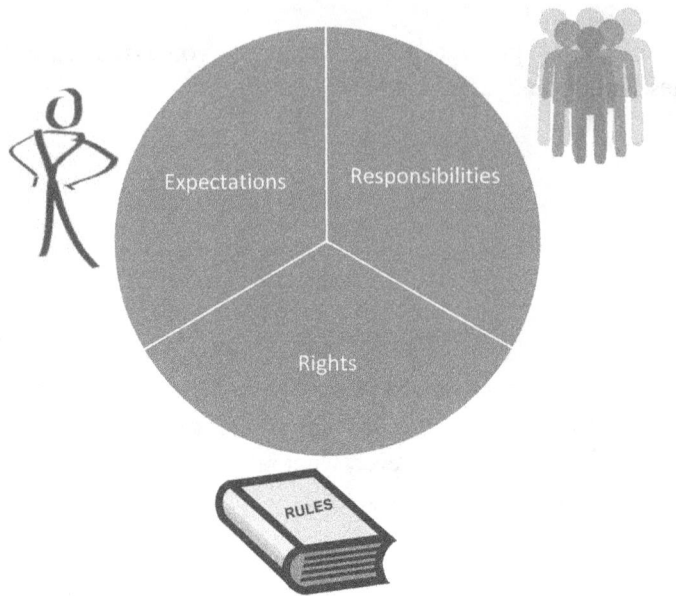

FIGURE 4.1
Culture of responsibility.

the question, "How can we rebuild the structures of our life together in pursuit of the common good?" He launched his journey by defining society as "the realm in which *all* of us is more important than *any* of us ... It is where we come together to achieve collectively what none of us can do alone."[3]

As he explored society-building through the centuries, Sacks referenced historical, political, and theological perspectives. Responsibility and freedom of choice were defining themes across all three disciplines. Sacks initially discussed responsibility as a matter of choice by an individual and how these small decisions impacted the larger society. He then expanded his exploration to global societies and how diverse groups would interconnect to begin building large, complex societies in which people chose to value the dignity of difference.

He coined the term "culture of responsibility" to categorize how different groups defined individual and collective accountability to group members and outsiders to manage change and create a social order. Individually based cultures build personal silos and all decisions focus on the self. Familial and tribal-based cultures develop specific rules and responsibilities that pertain to how people are treated within those communities and a separate set of rules and responsibilities for the treatment of people who come from outside the community.[4]

His analysis identified the most successful multi-cultural change agents as people who worked within a culture of responsibility and recognized they could only build a new society when they focused their efforts on the areas where they had power to control the outcome.[5] The 21st-century question is, how do we adapt the "us vs. them mentality"? Emotionally Intelligent leaders are able to guide people who come from diverse groups to work through the separateness of the other and merge responsibilities and foster constructive change that will help to achieve the community's goals.

CONSIDER AND DELIBERATE

Describe a situation (educational or professional) where you were part of the majority and someone from another type of culture was assigned to join your group.

How was the other person welcomed into your group?

Did anyone behave differently toward this person?

How would you describe the culture of responsibility demonstrated by the group?

Describe a time when you found yourself in a new cultural situation in which you were the other.

Was your first thought to escape, to blend in, or to hold onto the difference?

How did the people around you treat your "otherness"?

Did anyone offer you advice or social cues?

How long did it take for you to stop feeling like the other and feel like a member of the group?

When people build societies (organizations), all members of the founding group do not always share the same culture of responsibility. Prior experiences and traditions can make a difference. People observe that young children will play more easily with children who are different from them than adults. What is it that enables young children to be more accepting of the diversity of others than many adults? Perhaps it is because they have minimal life experience and no preconceptions which allow them to be more trusting and able to identify common ground more quickly. Adults don't have easy access to playgrounds and kickball fields; however, they can find common ground through conversation.

CHOICES AND CONVERSATION

People are described as accountable when they acknowledge their role in a decision and shoulder the consequences of any associated actions. Mistakes happen. The mark of an Emotionally Intelligent leader is what they do when these mistakes happen. Sometimes the people who must rectify the mistake had nothing to do with the cause. When this happens, how do people within your organization react? Do they say, "Not my fault, not my job to fix"? Or does your team come together to resolve the challenge with a broader focus? Taking responsibility to fix your mistake or to help someone else resolve a challenge is a choice.

Leadership and responsibility are defined by choices that people make. When I teach leadership classes, I use two examples about choice and responsibility that I learned from my children. The first involved my daughter when she was three years old. One morning, as I was trying to get us breakfast and out of the house, she spilled her milk. Spilling milk is what three-year-old children do. I sighed. I didn't yell. I simply sighed and went to get a paper towel. Emily was upset and blurted out, "I didn't make the spill!" I asked her who had spilled the milk since I was on the other side of the room. She said, "My hand did it." If I wasn't trying to get us out the door, I might have laughed at her fairly sound three-year-old logic. Instead, we were delayed as I explained her hand was connected to her body and that her brain controlled her body. So, although I wasn't angry that she spilled her milk, she needed to take responsibility for the spill and help me wipe it up. When people sidestep responsibility and try to blame someone else, I remember that long ago morning and silently think, "no your hand did not do it, be responsible." Emotionally Intelligent leaders do not look to point blame; they look for a solution to the situation.

The second story I share about responsibility and choice involves my son when he was 13 years old. He is a two-time Non-Hodgkin's Lymphoma survivor and underwent chemotherapy treatment between the ages of 10 and 14. Like many children diagnosed with cancer, he wanted to be a "normal" kid. We had many arguments about why he had to endure certain therapies to fight his cancer and we had arguments about why he had to complete his school work since he had cancer. He was pushing his boundaries just as any other adolescent.

He prepared for his Bar Mitzvah ceremony which marks the transition point for him to begin to assume adult ritual responsibilities. Part of his preparation was to write a speech that explained a lesson he learned from the weekly Torah portion. The section he chose to discuss described people who made a choice to become a servant to the priests within the ancient temple. He talked about this section and the responsibilities he would need to consider as he made choices as an adult Jew. He went on to explain, "I did not choose to get cancer, but I can choose how I behave now that I have cancer." Truly, I did not see the speech until after he had written it; however, as the adage goes … out of the mouth of babes. This teenager understood that even though he held no responsibility for the unpleasant situation where he found himself, he was fully empowered to take charge of his actions to move forward.

When diverse groups of people are brought together, everyone involved has a choice of how they will act. Psychologists talk about fight, flight, or freeze responses. So it is not unnatural for people to automatically jump into "us vs. them" confrontation mode when they haven't had a chance to develop trust among people who are merging into a new team. How much energy is wasted putting up antagonistic walls? After much time wasting, we finally let down our guard, loosen our bias, initiate conversations, and then discover we have much more in common than not.

Bruce Tuckman's "Forming, Storming, Norming, Performing" group development model accurately describes most team merging scenarios. My concern is, why do we need to spend so much time and energy within the Storming segment? Conversation is an undervalued tool that can help teams move quickly from the Forming to the Performing phase.

Initiating conversation enables people to explore their differences with dignity. It is a means of civil discourse that transforms potential confrontation into understanding and constructive action. Nadia Bolz-Weber, a Lutheran pastor, founded The House for All Sinners and Saints congregation in Denver, Colorado, and discovered the value of conversation to help people from different backgrounds find common ground.

Bolz-Weber founded her congregation to serve people who were not part of the stereotypical church-going populace. She brought spiritual grace to people who weren't comfortable attending mainstream churches. Tattoos and leather jackets were the norm among her congregants. She found herself in a quandary when mainstream folks wearing collared shirts and khakis began to attend services. She wasn't sure how to react to these newcomers, because she had launched her ministry to help people who often were shunned by mainstream people. In an odd thought reversal, she didn't appreciate these "others" attending the church she had built to support avant-garde lifestyles.

She sought counsel from a friend with a similar ministry who suggested she open her mind. She took the opportunity during a scheduled congregational meeting to discuss the purpose and mission of the church. The conversation that ensued between the two groups focused on what they hoped to gain through their church attendance. The original congregants realized that although they did not necessarily share similar lifestyles with the newcomers, they did share spiritual commonalities and could appreciate each other's differences. The congregation flourished amid diversity.[6]

CONSIDER AND DELIBERATE

Reflect back on preconceived expectations that turned out not to be as you expected in the following scenarios. Briefly note the object, person, or activity.

New Food –
Outdoor Activity or Outing –
Music/Theater Genre –
First Day at a New Job –
First Meeting with Temporary Assignment Team –

How many of these situations were positive experiences and how many were negative?

Did you need to overcome any extenuating challenges for these scenarios?

What commonalities existed between the varying experiences?

What risk level would you assign for each of these experiences?

In what way does the level of risk affect how you approach uncertainty?

Change is hard for many people. There can be great comfort in maintaining the status quo. If you are trying to initiate a change and find some people are hesitant to embrace your ideas, it is imperative for you to initiate a conversation to better understand their fears and concerns. You may find they didn't fully understand your explanation and once their questions are answered, they become proponents for your proposed action. Or, you might realize their reluctance is justified and they will join with you to develop a better solution. In either case, being able to facilitate a conversation is a valuable Emotionally Intelligent skill that enables all parties to gain an understanding of each other's needs, wants, strengths, and weaknesses so that they can unify their efforts to achieve their common goals.

USING CONVERSATION AS A GAP CLOSER

Pulling meaning out of conversation is determined by the commonality of language. Language is part of a culture that is defined by word usage, context, and tone. Ben Marcus, an American writer, made an interesting point when he wrote, "There are allegedly two stories to tell: a stranger comes to town, or a person went on a journey."[7] When people come together to create something larger than themselves they are starting a journey. They will need to depend on and cooperate with people who they may not know very well. What is scarier than heading into an unknown abyss with people who you have not yet learned to trust? Conversation provides the space for the language and interaction that will help you stop being strangers and come together to successfully find your way.

When people are brought together to form a working team, they bring a variety of expertise, experience, and jargon. Small misunderstandings can evolve into major standoffs because people are using words that might have different meanings to different people. Most people want the work effort to be successful; they simply are used to performing the work differently or using different terminology. Because the procedure or jargon is outside their comfort zone, people become afraid that they will be negatively judged and shut down. Emotionally Intelligent leaders develop skills they use to guide people through the process of creating a common language so each member of the group is able to communicate their message so that it is received with the meaning they intended.

Growing up mixed race in South Africa, Trevor Noah discovered the power a common language can provide when people who don't know each other focus on the obvious differences. He spoke several languages and learned that speaking with other people in their dialect was a tremendous tool to help him avoid trouble. People would speak with their friends not expecting Noah to understand their words, much less be fluent in their native tongue. Undaunted, he would calmly join in their conversation in his "simulcast" mode mimicking their exact dialect and intonation. Hearing someone who did not look like them speaking with the same inflection and jargon as they did caught them off guard, but within moments they started speaking with Noah as if he was one of their group.[8]

CONVERSATIONS AND VIRTUAL TEAMS

The challenge for 21st-century leaders is how to align, motivate, and coordinate efforts of people who are not co-located and may never have met face-to-face. Managers and leaders must develop a more complex set of skills to connect and align people who are dispersed across geography and time zones. The differences multiple languages and regional dialects bring to a global workplace are intensified when teams work virtually. No one is right or wrong—just different—until the working group can agree on a common procedure and understand each other's jargon.

Creating virtual connections and strong relationships among dispersed team members is the sign of a strong leader. How do remotely located managers discover, share, and combine the strengths of their reporting teams? How do they motivate their staff and monitor work activities from afar? These work environments require leaders to demonstrate exemplary communication skills. If your team understands the group mission and how their work efforts align with the organization's goals, they will not buckle at the monitoring and reporting activities that are needed to ensure milestones and related tasks are synchronized with budget, resource, and schedule expectations.

Virtual team leadership requires a tremendous amount of collaborative activity. A single person cannot create a virtual community by themselves. A virtual community can only happen through the collaborative efforts of everyone involved. Leaders who take the extra time to connect virtual teams and build trust among the dispersed team members will see measurable business results from their efforts.

CONSIDER AND DELIBERATE

Describe a time when you worked with a group of people who were not co-located.

How did you establish a sense of trust?

How did this group communicate and track work efforts?

What was the most challenging aspect for you as a member of this virtual work team?

Leaders are responsible for setting and modeling effective virtual communication norms. Patience, persistence, and direct one-to-one conversations using email, video meetings, phone calls, and other communication platforms will maximize team performance and minimize misunderstandings.

When I worked for an international software company, I discovered during a conversation with a European colleague how severely behind schedule an announced software release had become. Between us, we worked out a solution in which he borrowed two of my staff resources. The cross-Atlantic collaborative team worked together to reduce the estimated nine-month delay to one week past the original release date. This was a tremendous accomplishment that would never have happened if we had not worked at developing a virtual relationship based on trusted communications. I cannot overemphasize how important a tool conversation is for Emotionally Intelligent leaders who need to mediate conflict caused by misunderstandings among team members whether people are co-located or working virtually.

OVER-COMMUNICATING

Some leaders resort to "over-communicating" by sending multiple messages to dispersed team members. When they don't respond as desired, they get angry and start blasting multiple communications and addressing more people than necessary. If people are non-responsive to your messages and you've sent a reminder, don't blame your people for bad behavior. Take a moment and review the message you are sending. Is it clear and concise? Do you need to read through paragraphs of verbiage to get to the task assignment or request? Do you use the message header line to succinctly identify the topic?

Remember, when communicating with people who may have different communication styles:

- Describe the purpose of the communication in the email header or agenda title
- Keep the message simple and brief
- Attach necessary documents
- Share appropriate links for background information and resources
- Arrange for a meeting to clarify and confirm understanding

MEETING MANAGEMENT

Managing meetings is a difficult skill to master. Have you experienced meetings that were a (1) waste of time, (2) too long, or (3) unorganized? Providing an agenda with time allocations in advance and the expectation that people will come prepared to discuss the topics is a simple success strategy. During the meeting, assign someone to track time and call a stop when the agenda topic discussion goes beyond the allocated time. To keep the meeting on track, suggest a separate meeting be scheduled to give the topic the needed attention. Assuring that the meeting attendees are cognizant of time allotments ensures all agenda topics are discussed before the meeting ends.

It is not unusual for people to complain that they sat through a long meeting for which they made no contribution. What if it were possible to change the traditional "time-wasting" meeting structure? Do all meetings need to be scheduled for one or two hours? Do all people need to be in every meeting?

Consider scheduling shorter meetings with fewer people and a tight agenda. You, as the group leader, would schedule 10- to 20-minute meetings with the people directly associated with a single agenda item. Although your schedule allocates two hours for meetings, your staff can be more productive because they only participate in the meetings for the topics that directly relate to their work.

```
┌─────────────────────────┐
│  T-POINT Agenda         │
│   • Thank               │
│   • Purpose             │
│   • Outline             │
│   • INput               │
│   • Transition          │
└─────────────────────────┘
```

FIGURE 4.2
T-POINT meeting agenda.

One tool that helps to keep meetings on track is the T-POINT agenda format. Figure 4.2 summarizes this meeting management method. Begin every meeting (whether 2 or 200 participants) by thanking everyone for attending and being prepared to participate in the discussion. State the purpose of the meeting to help people focus on the outcome. The meeting outline is a list of discussion topics and the time allocated for each one. The input section is the working part of the meeting. Lastly, time should be allocated for transition that identifies action items and, if needed, the next meeting.

CULTURE, CONVERSATION, AND COLLABORATION

The key to successful communication and conversations is to use nonjudgmental language. An authentic, even tone will help you clarify facts and intent while maintaining a position of strength and calm. All viewpoints can be discussed and evaluated with the hopes of coming to some type of constructive agreement that enables the group to move forward. Listening skills, respect, and a desire to learn how others view the situation are the keys to creating trust across organizational, geographic, and cultural divides.

Culture is an interesting dynamic, whether you are collaborating within the same location or across many miles. Growing up, the golden rule that said "do unto others as you would have them do unto you" was drilled into me as the hallmark of basic respect. Recently, people discuss the platinum rule that recommends that we consider treating people how they prefer to be treated.

Behavior we consider respectful may or may not be respectful based on someone else's culture, ethnic, or religious norms. There may be a brief overly polite "after you, no after you" shuffle as people from different organizational cultures work through the protocols that work best for them;

however, the respect they develop through this process will go a long way toward fostering trust and the ensuing collaborative efforts.

The term "culture" can reference personal workstyle or organizational work environment as well as ethnic or religious norms. Have you had difficulties working with other people, but could not figure out why you couldn't get along? Work styles have caused conflict since the time of hunters and gatherers. So whether the diversity of your team is based on ethnic, generational, personality, or work style traits, leaders need to help their teams recognize each other's strengths and enable them to learn how to come together to create a strong team effort.

A few questions you may want to ask yourself when comparing your workstyle to that of another person include:

- Are you an introvert or an extrovert?
- Are you an early morning person or do you work more productively later in the day?
- Do you prefer just the facts or do you think like a spider web?
- Do you need to document every conversation or wait to summarize the final decision?
- Do you prefer brainstorming solutions or do you prefer to reflect on a challenge before having a discussion?
- Are you comfortable communicating primarily via technology or do you prefer a more personal touch?

Some people make a generational distinction with regard to work styles and approach to colleagues within a work environment. However, please be careful resorting to stereotypes because all of the above personality traits and working styles can be found among baby boomers, millennials, gen-Xers, gen-Zers, etc.

CONSIDER AND DELIBERATE

Reflect on a time when you did not think you would get along with someone, but by the end of the project you had developed a professional friendship.

What were your initial thoughts about this person?

Was there a specific moment that changed the direction of your relationship?

How did you describe that person when the project ended?

Workstyles will change based on your experience, work environments, timelines, and other activities you are juggling in your personal and professional lives. Others also will adapt their workstyles over time. It is important to avoid thinking that people will not change and observe their current behavior before providing a response based on your past experiences.

CONVERSATIONAL FEEDBACK

Conversation is a two-way process that enables people to summarize alternatives being considered and explain their thought process. Feedback is a process that begins with someone describing how another person and their actions are perceived. Less than stellar feedback sessions usually end as one-way data streams. When the person providing the feedback allows the receiver to ask questions and explain any misconceptions, the feedback session becomes a constructive conversation.

For many people, the concept of inviting people to share perspectives and provide feedback to your thoughts is a scary situation. Collaborative conversations do not always happen easily. Trust may not have fully developed. People may be concerned about sharing information among teammates with whom they've never worked before. Or, they may be worried about sounding "stupid" to new colleagues. To encourage productive collaborative sessions among newly formed groups, a facilitator can help the group explore possibilities. The Collaborative SCHOLAR Conversational Model[9] illustrated in Figure 4.3 is a facilitation tool that can help the

SCHOLAR
Collaborative Conversation Model

Collaborative Value	Suggested Statement Sample
Scrutinize	Analyze strengths/weaknesses of current reality
Connect	Reach out through the organization
Hone	Evaluate short- and long-term vision
Options	Brainstorm, review, and evaluate
Leverage	Available assets
Accountable	Own your actions

FIGURE 4.3

Collaborative SCHOLAR conversation model.

working groups explore boundaries and options which may not otherwise be considered.

The acronym SCHOLAR identifies a seven-step process to facilitate innovative problem solving. Each of the seven steps takes your team from an initial conversation that defines a common understanding of the starting point, the solution development phase, and the change management procedures. Reality may cause you to refine the solution plan. Simply, use the collaborative process to retool and adapt the original plan to create the final solution.

The *Scrutinize* step encourages your working group to analyze the current situation. Document the assets you have working in your favor and document those challenges that could impede your progress. The *Connect* step encourages reaching out into other areas of your organization that might have needed expertise or experience. The *Hone* step suggests you break your vision into short- and long-term goals. Being able to introduce smaller successes may help other people in your organization to gain confidence and more fully support your ultimate purpose. The *Options* step is a time to think about alternative ways to accomplish your goal. Once people start to review and evaluate alternatives, some ideas may be discarded; however, an idea that has never before been deployed may be the launch point for an award-winning solution. The *Leverage* step encourages people to review existing resources that are underutilized or can be repurposed.

The final two steps are the most important for leaders to remember. *Be Accountable* and own your actions. Share all of the positive credit with your group members. When the work effort provides a less-than-positive experience, you should assume responsibility for the misstep. Share the lessons learned as feedback so that you and your team won't make similar mistakes in the future. Lastly, be aware that nothing is permanent. Environmental conditions will change and you will need to *Refine* your approach. Be ready to help your team learn from mistakes, adapt, and continue forward.

This chapter described some of the considerations Emotionally Intelligent leaders consider when they lead an effort to create a collaborative culture that provides a supportive workplace where people are encouraged to work together to successfully develop innovative solutions. The next chapter explores how to leverage the diversity of people's work styles to create a positive and productive workplace.

NOTES

1 Grant, Adam. (2016). *Originals.* (pp. 180–181). New York, NY: Penguin Books.
2 Grant, Adam. (2016). *Originals.* (pp. 251). New York, NY: Penguin Books.
3 Sacks, Jonathan. (2007). *The Home We Build Together—Recreating Society.* (pp. 4–5). London, England: Continuum.
4 Sacks, Jonathan. (2007). *The Home We Build Together—Recreating Society.* (pp. 132–133). London, England: Continuum.
5 Sacks, Jonathan. (2007). *The Home We Build Together—Recreating Society.* (p. 133). London, England: Continuum. Sacks, Jonathan.
6 Tippett, Krista. On Being. (October 23, 2014). "Seeing the Underside and Seeing God: Tattoos, Tradition, and Grace."
7 Marcus, Ben. (2004). The Anchor Book of New American Short Stories. (p. xii). New York, NY: Anchor Books.
8 Noah, Trevor. (2016). Born a Crime. (pp. 55–56). New York, NY: Spiegel & Grau.
9 ©2017 by Susan Schwartz of the River Birch Group. Reprinted with permission.

CHAPTER SUMMARY

The Power of Collaboration and Conversation

- Strong leaders help collaborative teams identify their unique capabilities and integrate the efforts of all the participants into a collaborative force to achieve the shared vision.
- A measure of successful collaboration is defined by how teams are able to develop collective responsibilities to adapt inherited cultures to meet the needs of the evolving community.
- Conversation is a tool that enables people to avoid confrontation and begin to gain an understanding of each other's needs, wants, strengths, and weaknesses in order to unify their efforts to achieve common goals.
- Collaborative conversation is a powerful process that can be used by diverse working groups to promote innovative problem solving.

5

Workplace Diversity

> Different workstyles are...
> Collaborative workspaces assure...
> Constructive feedback enables leaders to...

Pierre Teilhard de Chardin, a French Jesuit and paleontologist, prophesied, "The coming age of evolution won't be driven by physical adaptation, but by human consciousness, creativity, and spirit." The astonishing aspect of this quote is that de Chardin was born at the start of the scientifically driven industrial revolution and lived through the development of major 20th-century inventions: motor cars, radio, airplanes. A common value of this era was that machines would drive the progress of man. Yet, he puts his confidence in the capabilities of man.

De Chardin began his scientific career in China, where he worked with the team that discovered the Peking Man. Through his studies, he recognized the role physical adaptation and evolution played in man's early development. Mid-career, he switched his studies to philosophy in order to explore modern man's thought processes. He was especially interested in how the sharing of ideas could help evolutionary adaptation. He did not believe innovation could occur within a vacuum. He proved through his research that group discussion was the core foundation responsible for human survival. He visualized a cyclical thought process which centered on people deliberating and debating ideas. One person builds on another person's ideas until a practical reality is created that might never have been practiced before.[1]

DOI: 10.1201/9781003520719-5

In the same vein, Emotionally Intelligent leaders identify and leverage the individual strengths of people with diverse work styles to create something bigger than they could have created on their own. Team leaders, who are able to recognize the varying experiences that different people bring to a challenge, are already several steps ahead of the manager who assumes there is only one way to resolve an issue. Success is dependent on a team's ability to foster collaborative group discussions that enable all members to share, comment, and adapt ideas. A single loud voice insisting there is only one way to resolve the situation only considers the perspective of one person. Collaborative discussions incorporate a variety of viewpoints which manipulate, twist, and reshape thoughts to create an innovative solution.

CONSIDER AND DELIBERATE

Describe a situation in either your personal or professional life when you and other people were stymied by an unexpected challenge.

What caused the process/project/activity to stall?

How did the situation become "unstuck"? Did a single person save the day or was it a group effort?

Could the problem situation have been prevented? How?

What lessons learned did you take from the situation?

The best ideas always seem to surface when the group has run out of standard solutions. People begin to toss around impossible suggestions and suddenly someone will say, "Wait, that just might work." The group then begins to refine the outlandish suggestion until a workable solution is finalized.

COLLABORATIVE WORKING GROUPS

Working relationships among team members will adjust over time. Emotionally Intelligent people try out different voices and take on a variety of leading and supporting roles while they pursue various collaborative efforts. Assignments will broaden as people discover skills and expertise they may never have realized they, or others, possessed. Unofficial roles may be assumed by people who are particularly good at networking throughout the organization, those who plan celebrations, those who simplify complicated situations, or those who are particularly good at note taking, editing, or fact checking. Emotionally Intelligent leaders pay attention to these shifts and adjust motivators, recognition, and success metrics to mirror the expanding productivity of the group and individual team members.

The Corporate Executive Board (CEB), a best practice insight and technology company, initiated a global, cross-industry study of 1,440 customer service representatives in 2015. The data culled from the study identified seven discrete personality types to describe the people who performed contact center functions, as well as the associated level of effectiveness for each personality type who performed as a help desk service rep. The seven personality types identified by the study continue to be relevant. They are:

- The Controller
- The Rock

- The Accommodator
- The Empathizer
- The Hard Worker
- The Innovator
- The Competitor

As might be expected, the largest group of individuals (32%) identified as an Empathizer which is described as someone who is an empathetic listener. However, the people who identified as a Controller (15%) were recognized as providing the most efficient and pain-free customer service. The report describes a Controller as someone with strong opinions and who likes to demonstrate their knowledge. Basically, they are skilled at confidently telling people what to do and how to do it—and they enjoy doing so.[2]

The results from the CEB front line service representatives study are not so surprising with regard to the current focus of customer service organizations. The data's value is that it demonstrates a microcosm of the anecdotal collaborative team referenced throughout this book. Table 5.1 defines each of the seven roles as defined by the study. The rightmost column is included so you can reflect on the various representations of each personality type

TABLE 5.1

Working Group Roles

Call Center Representative Team Role	General Behaviors	CEB Study Percentage	Your Organization
The Controller	Likes to share opinions and direct group activities	15%	
The Rock	Maintains optimism and calm in all situations	12%	
The Accommodator	Brings many voices into decision and works for people to meet halfway	11%	
The Empathizer	Listens carefully and enjoys helping others resolve issues	32%	
The Hard Worker	Insists on following procedures and adheres to deadlines	20%	
The Innovator	Enjoys creating new methods to enhance established procedures	9%	
The Competitor	Focuses on goal achievement and views activities as win/lose opportunities	1%	

within your organization team. Additional rows are inserted for you to use to identify any additional personality types that may be unique to your team.

Every working group is made up of a blend of the roles identified in Table 5.1. Depending on the organizational function performed, the percentages of the people who represent the different roles will vary. For example, solution-based sales teams will have a significant percentage of people who identify as a Competitor. However, this does not mean that only Competitors work in a sales-related function. Every sales team is made up of people who identify and perform the function of one of the described roles. Collaborative teams are most successful when different members are able to analyze a situation from a variety of perspectives.

CONSIDER AND DELIBERATE

Looking back on the past three years, list the different professional and personal groups for which you have been a member. Next to each group, identify the role(s) listed in Table 5.1 that you played within that group environment.

To the best of your recollection, how were the seven roles represented among your colleagues over the course of these different group experiences? Was there a significant percentage of one type of role or an even distribution?

Which group experience did you enjoy the most? Why?

Which group experience did you enjoy the least? Why?

Did you perform the same functional role(s) during each?

Out of all the roles you listed, which one do you find you naturally gravitate toward?

People will take on different roles when working within different team environments and may even shift their participatory role on longer term projects as they gain skills and take on responsibilities of people who move on to other projects. No role is "better" than another role. Each one contributes to the total effort. In fact, it might prove beneficial to encourage team members to switch their natural roles within the team for a day to encourage broader perspective and innovation.

CULTURE AND COLLABORATIVE GROUPS

Colonel Scott A. Jackson shared an interesting U.S. Army cultural tradition which follows the absorption process of the entry-level lieutenant into a fully operational working unit. This entry officer level often oversees non-commissioned officers who have many years of experience. A young officer must prove he is worthy of the soldier's respect. The Lieutenant title does not guarantee a young officer automatic respect. The orientation process begins with the announcement that "a" lieutenant has been assigned to the unit. When the young officer arrives, they are referred to as "the" Lieutenant. Senior officers know the young officer has established trust and become fully integrated into the unit operations when the reporting soldiers refer to them as "our" Lieutenant.[3]

I had a similar experience working with my seasoned technicians at AT&T. The day they stopped calling me "Susan" and started calling me "Schwartzy," I knew I was considered part of their team since they only called their trusted team members by their last names. Giving me a nickname was their way of telling me that I was doing more than okay.

The culture of trust within the group determines the roles that different members play. Often the culture described by organizational leaders may not actually be the culture people experience day to day. Edgar Schein, a noted scholar of organization development, observed that in every organization there are three different cultural levels (Figure 5.1). The Artifacts layer is made up of promotions that define the organization's publicly seen image. These can be legends or a visual image such as the building's architectural façade.

The Shared Values level represents what the organization leadership says they are or would like to be. This is the level that contains the strategies, goals, and philosophies that provide the foundation for the organization's business practices.

The Shared Assumptions level is what the people within the organization experience on a daily basis. Schein describes this level as being where the unconscious perceptions of the organization's management and staff are found. This is the actual working culture of the organization.[4]

The actual working culture of an organization can be an unexpected positive or negative. Have you ever been assigned to work with someone described as a "difficult" client or manager and discovered you worked

FIGURE 5.1
Cultural organizational levels.

well with them? The dreaded assignment turned into a golden opportunity for you to learn and build skills. On the other hand, have you ever accepted a position only to discover that your actual duties are different from what was described in the position description and interview process? Were you ever told you were being hired for your skills and creativity only to discover that the only "good" ideas belong to your supervising manager? When you query your team members for counsel because you believe you discovered a problem, they tell you to keep quiet and do as you're told. It does not matter what the company logo or strategic plan espouses, the culture of a working group is determined by the actual daily work culture.

CREATING A COLLABORATIVE ENVIRONMENT

When people are afraid to speak up because they are afraid of being belittled, or possibly punished, they will nod in agreement even though they know there is essential information that should be considered. They simply want to survive unscathed from any retribution from the person who wants to control the discussion and group outcome. Innovative ideas that could decrease costs, improve operations, or increase sales are lost because people are too fearful of the repercussions that occur when people disagree with the strongest voice in the room.

James Detert and Ethan Burris identified common management pitfalls demonstrated by even the best-intentioned leaders that can prevent people from speaking up when they have concerns. These challenges are categorized within two areas: fear factors and futility factors. One practice they identified as fear factor inducing is the practice of relying on anonymous feedback. Although industry best practices have used anonymity as a means to encourage open and honest feedback, it actually inhibits frank discussions that can lead to problem resolutions. Instead of encouraging people to bring concerns forward, these anonymous suggestion boxes are actually sending the subliminal message, "It's not safe to share your views openly in this organization."

The second cause for concern regarding the practice of anonymity they discovered is that when negative feedback was channeled via the suggestion box, it was not uncommon for management to pursue a debilitating witch hunt to determine who perpetrated the negative feedback. The employees in these organizations will definitely think twice before they place any future negative feedback into the comment box.

Their third concern with using anonymity practices is that, without knowing the source of concern, people may take the original premise out of context which can create a larger problem since the message originator is not available to more fully explain their comments. Or, in the case of anonymous messages reporting abusive behavior, appropriate measures cannot be taken to rectify the situation since the HR Ombudsman cannot initiate action without being able to speak with someone to start the formal exploratory process. If the accusation is specific enough, the manager will recognize the person and possibly take further abusive action.

Other instances that might be categorized as a fear factor inducer are the result of managers who say they have an open door policy, but will not consider any comments or feedback regarding projects for which they are the lead or heavily involved. Body language may also prevent people from sharing feedback. The authors suggest managers be cognizant of "power" postures. For example, leaning back from behind a large desk may seem to present a relaxing environment to staff; however, it establishes a power divide—more like being on opposite sides of a stream which doesn't encourage collaborative, peer-based conversation. Gathering around a table where everyone is sitting in similar chairs will promote more open discussions.

When people take the time to provide input and then are not included in the final report or presentation without explanation, they are being told that their efforts are not meaningful. There could be very good reasons the information was not included, but if these folks are not provided an explanation, they may not be quite as willing to provide support in the future. This is what the authors mean by a futility factor. Sometimes people will say that what they received was not what they asked the person to prepare, there was no time for correction, and so they could not include the person's work. Managers need to ensure that they provide people with specific directions and, if possible, examples of the desired format, to eliminate any uncertainty regarding deliverables.

Emotionally Intelligent leaders encourage a constructive feedback culture by incorporating feedback as part of daily casual conversation. People will become accustomed to sharing ideas without feeling as if they are being put on the spot. Other suggestions, the authors mention include being transparent when priorities or budgets change. You may not believe it is appropriate to share the specific details that went into the necessary change, but a certain amount of transparency will help to mitigate any futility that people might be feeling. By sharing the challenges that came up during executive discussions, they will believe that you did your best to present their viewpoints and concerns. Whether the action is about a decision not to include a chart in a presentation or to stop a significant work effort, Emotionally Intelligent leaders take the time to close the loop with a constructive conversation letting the people on their team know that they and their work are appreciated and valued.[5]

CONSIDER AND DELIBERATE

Select an organization you've worked within professionally or as a volunteer. Briefly outline the culture based on the Schein's three-level model: Artifacts, Shared Values, and Shared Assumptions.

Do the three levels align? If not, where did the disconnect occur?

How did the alignment or nonalignment affect your experience?

Based on your reflections, how did the leaders of the group inhibit or promote fear and futility factors among the working group members?

One of an Emotionally Intelligent leader's superpowers is their ability to communicate an organization's message and mission with the intention to create a positively energized workplace.

MATTERING AT WORK

The U.S. Surgeon General's Office published a framework for workplace mental health and wellbeing in the American workplace in November 2022. One of the five essential elements identified to support a healthy supportive workplace that engages workers is "Mattering at Work." This element describes a respectful workplace where workers understand how their work contributes to the mission purpose of the organization.[6] What I find most interesting is that in order for a person to believe that they and their work matter, they need to hear a manager or colleague say that they value them and their work.

External validation is essential for a person to matter. I know that I and my work matter when someone offers me a genuine compliment because they confirmed my value. Just as easily, when people offer me a proforma response, ignore, or discount my efforts they are telling me that my work has no value. If it happens often enough, I begin to believe I am incompetent and will never play a significant role within any workplace. When a person feels "dematterized," they begin to disengage from workplace activities. They isolate themselves from other group members, their performance drops, and they leave to work for another organization.

For example, my friend Alice worked 18 hours a day for 9 months to meet an unrealistic project timeframe. The program manager was happy and appreciative of Alice's abilities and commitment. Shortly after the work was completed, Alice received a poor performance review. Her reviewer did not speak with the program manager about the project challenges or Alice's role. They wrote that Alice had poor time management skills and needed to prioritize her work more effectively. A less than 5-minute conversation between the reviewing manager and Alice de-matterized a highly skilled, global IT professional. She began to perform at the bare minimum of expectations and eventually took a position with another company.

Unfortunately, my friend Alice is not an anomaly. Gallup's *State of the Global Workplace: 2023 Report* estimates disengaged employee behavior costs the global economy $8.8 trillion dollars in lost productivity due to high turnover, poor performance, and increased absenteeism.[7] Emotionally Intelligent leaders who create positive workplace cultures can reverse this trend. Gallup followed several organizations that implemented low-cost employee engagement programs that:

- Connected individual work with organizational mission
- Engaged workers in workplace decisions
- Built a culture of gratitude and recognition

These Emotionally Intelligent actions promote respect and actively engage employees and provide significant business results. After one year, the employee engagement programs, observed by the Gallup team, increased retention rates by 22%, decreased absenteeism by 44%, and increased profits by 11%.[8]

CONSIDER AND DELIBERATE

Describe a time when a manager's action gave you confidence.

Describe a time when a manager's action devalued you and your work.

What were the differences between these two different situations?

THE CULTURE OF MATRIX TEAMS

Matrix organization structures often are used as the first step to integrate previously separate organizations. This first step toward a larger organizational change offers a leader an enormous opportunity. The challenge is how to align the current cultures of the working groups

A common management error is to ignore the differences and assume that everyone will immediately adapt and wear the new corporate uniform with pride. People are not robots. It is part of human nature to want to have some control over our destiny. The most successful change and merger efforts are driven from within the affected working groups. Leaders did not drive the change; instead, they empowered individuals to create the change needed to get their groups to the desired destination.

The first steps to organizational integration often begin with cross-functional teams that are created by the overseeing managers "borrowing" people from other units within the organization. The benefits of "borrowing" people include the opportunity to introduce a variety of experiences and perspectives that can help to drive innovation while minimizing costs and redundant operations. However, the dynamics of merging different work groups can be difficult. Staff members will have conflicting priorities when choosing how to align themselves—the "dotted-line" manager or the person who completes their performance review?

Balancing the complexities of a matrix team environment is a practical challenge for everyone involved. The team leader must corral diverse personalities, multiple reporting structures, and varying performance expectations to develop a synchronized group of people. Successful matrix team leaders need to be able to keep everyone's focus on the alignment of the group and organizational goals. They must recognize different work styles, minimize competing objectives, and synchronize resource coordination and communications. If they can achieve this delicate balance, the broader perspectives and diverse experiences fostered by matrix team alignments can provide great value to the organization and participating individuals.

DIVERSITY OF COMMUNICATION WORKSTYLES

Many workplace difficulties are rooted in simple misunderstandings. When people take the time to work through interpersonal conflicts, the ultimate cause is most often attributed to different communication styles and expectations. Being able to recognize and adapt to other people's communication needs is an essential skill for all people, especially those who work within a matrix organization environment.

There are a number of workplace assessment and profile tools to help teams understand each other's work styles with the intention of improving communications and productivity. Some of the most popular of these assessment tools are Myers-Briggs Type Indicator®, EQ-I 2.0®, and DiSC®. The DiSC® profile categorizes people as one of four types: Driver, Influencer, Steadiness, and Conscientious. Table 5.2 addresses

TABLE 5.2

DISC Communication Style Profiles

	Driver	**Influencer**	**Steadiness**	**Conscientious**
Attribute	Direct	Enthusiastic	Calm	Careful
	Fast Decisions	Optimistic	Deliberate	Systematic
Limits	Impatient	Impulsive	Indecisive	Over-analyzes
	Skeptical	Disorganized		
Fears	Being Seen as Vulnerable	Being Ignored	Change	Criticism
Communication Requirements	Bottom Line	Ask Questions	Clarification	Focus on Facts
Needs Others To:	Weigh Pros & Cons	Focus on Facts	React Quickly to Change	Compromise
	Research Facts	Have a Systematic Approach	Apply Pressure to Others	Encourage Teamwork

the traditional DiSC® identity profiles from a communications perspective. If you are not familiar with DiSC® profiles, the first four rows will help you identify the different workstyle tendencies for you and your colleagues. The lower four rows compare the communication preferences and needs for each profile.

By understanding your co-workers' limitations and fears, you can provide the supportive tasks identified in the final row. You may even find that your impossible boss may not be quite so impossible, if you are able to adjust your communication style to best meet their needs.

Personally, I am an Influencer and think like a spider web. I work through all kinds of scenarios and want to share them all. Over the years, I have worked for several managers who would be identified as Drivers. I was in my 20s when I worked for my first Driver manager. It was not a positive experience for me. Reflecting back, I expected him to adapt his style to support me. It was an immature viewpoint and I paid a political price. Mid-career, when I encountered another Driver manager, I had matured as a manager and was able to view situations from a broader perspective. I recognized my manager's need to be presented with the essential decision points while being prepared with backup data to answer questions. My work life became much easier once I understood how my manager's work style differed from mine and I was able to adapt my workstyle to best support my manager.

CONSIDER AND DELIBERATE

Referencing the DiSC® communications style table above, which work style do you believe best describes you?

Think about someone who you would characterize as a difficult person. Which work style do you think best describes them?

How can you adapt your behavior to change the dynamics and hopefully improve your working relationship?

Whether your organization is a small business, global corporation, government agency, a non-profit group, or a volunteer community group, people make the difference between success or failure. Emotionally Intelligent leaders are able to pay attention and respond appropriately to varying workstyle and communication needs to motivate people so they can perform at their highest capabilities.

WORKSTYLES AND TEAM TASKS

Independent of their personal preference, people will need to perform a variety of tasks within a team environment. Sometimes one person may take the lead and at other times they will focus on completing a specific task. Emotionally Intelligent leaders watch closely to make sure that each team member takes on task types that will leverage their capabilities, incorporate professional growth opportunities, and move the team toward the designated goal.

Meredith Belbin, an industrial psychologist, developed a Team Role theory that organizes team functions into three task categories:

- *Action-oriented*
- *People-oriented*
- *Thought-oriented*

Action-oriented task roles represent the doers who work to complete the specific work activities to achieve the goal. The people-oriented task roles represent the person within the group who is well-networked and always seems to know someone who knows someone who could provide information or some other kind of assistance. Thought-oriented task roles represent people who are able to provide the group a view of the larger picture such as subject-matter specialists, quality monitors, and resource managers. Most people will perform all three types of task roles at different times depending on the project and other team member skills.

Expanding Belbin's theory to a leadership perspective, a person might find themself taking on a leadership type of task role even when they have not officially been designated the leader. Or, designated leaders may find themselves performing a specific worker-bee type function. Flexibility is a strong attribute for leaders to possess. Each task that builds toward achieving the designated goal is important.

Egos cannot get in the way. If a task needs doing and everyone on the team is constructively engaged, roll up your sleeves and attend to the requirement at hand. When your team sees you pitching in to help with mundane jobs, they quickly see the importance of what they might have considered a menial task and are more motivated to work harder to achieve the shared team goals.

An example of just such a situation involved my son, Carl, who was training to be a chef with Executive Chef Bryan Voltaggio at his fine dining restaurant Volt in Frederick, Maryland. This was the summer Voltaggio opened his first Family Meal restaurant. Although Carl had the late shift, which involved cleaning and closing the Volt fine dining kitchen, he had been told to be at the Family Meal kitchen early to deep-clean the refrigerator in preparation for the new restaurant opening. Needless to say, Carl was not a happy worker. When he reported to work in the morning, the only other person in the kitchen was Bryan Voltaggio, the executive chef and owner. The two of them worked together to get the job done. Carl realized that deep-cleaning the refrigerator was essential to running a restaurant, and not a menial task to assign to the most junior team member. The conversation they shared while they scrubbed offered my son a unique mentoring opportunity.

CONSIDER AND DELIBERATE

Consider a recent work effort you performed as part of a group. What tasks/responsibilities did you perform as part of the work effort?

Can you assign each of these tasks/responsibilities to the appropriate category?

Action-Oriented:

People-Oriented:

Thought-Oriented:

Select another work effort you performed as part of a group. What tasks/responsibilities did you perform as part of the work effort?

Can you assign each of these tasks/responsibilities to the appropriate category?

Action-Oriented:

People-Oriented:

Thought-Oriented:

How did the roles you performed during the first work effort compare to the roles you performed as part of the second work effort?

Which roles did you enjoy performing most? Why?

Shifting between action, people, and thought-oriented task roles provides many benefits. Emotionally Intelligent leaders should exercise different working muscles. Sharing broad perspectives will help team members develop new skills and establish stronger relationships with other team members which will enhance productivity for the entire work group.

COACHING FOR PERFORMANCE

A leader's effectiveness can be measured by the quality of the people they develop and succession planning that has been put into place. When a senior leader brags about their indispensability to the organization, it really means they have not trained anyone to take on his/her responsibilities. Yes, they are indispensable; so indispensable in fact, they cannot be considered for promotion since they have not trained a successor.

Dr. Henry Cloud defines a leader's role as "the creation of the kinds of conditions in which people can bring their brains, gifts, hearts, talents, and energy to the realization of a vision."[9] Strong leaders are lifelong learners and provide opportunities for people working with them to do so. They are the people who help people realize that they are part of a whole that is greater than the immediate cubicle walls.

When I think back to the leaders who most influenced me, I recall the moments when they helped me to think through the challenge that needed resolving. At that moment in time, I just wanted them to tell me what to do. However, coaching me to identify the "real" issue and work through the possibilities for resolution was a great gift. It might have been easier to tell me what to do; but, taking the time to coach me through the decision process was the right thing to do.

Jorgen Vig Knudstorp was asked about the strongest leadership lesson he learned during his 15-year tenure as Lego's Chief Executive Officer. He responded, "Thank you for doing all the things I never told you to do. You shouldn't run a company based on what you tell employees to do. You should run it based on intention." He clarified his comment by explaining "context-setting was more important than controlling." His strategy was to outline a vision and create an environment that empowered his staff to take the needed action to achieve the vision. The success of this strategy is demonstrated by the company's turnaround effort that took Lego from a negative cash flow position to the leading global toy manufacturer.[10]

The following checklist may prove helpful as you work toward creating the conditions which will empower your team to pursue the needed action to achieve success.

- Sustain Mutual Respect and Purpose
- Be Open to Hear the Truth
- Assure Safety of Conversation
- Listen for Multiple Perspectives
- Ask Exploratory Questions to Clarify
- Enhance Relationships

Below are a series of questions that can help you identify your strengths and growth areas for you and your organization.

- **Sustain Mutual Respect and Purpose**
  - Do you and your team members understand how your assignment aligns with the overall organization mission?
  - Are you modeling respectful behavior?
  - How are you handling disrespectful behaviors on your team?
- **Be Open to Hear the Truth**
  - Do people only share positive feedback with you?
  - How is negative feedback or other examples of staff concerns handled?
- **Assure Safety of Conversation**
  - How often does your team engage in casual conversation?
  - Are you open to constructive feedback?
- **Listen for Multiple Perspectives**
  - Do you discuss potential consequences of an action with the people who will be affected by your decision?
  - When was the last time you considered a challenging situation from more than your personal perspective?
- **Ask Explanatory Questions to Clarify**
  - When people come to you for advice, do you immediately provide an answer or do you ask questions to confirm your understanding of the request?
  - During your last team meeting, how many times did you respond to a query with a clarifying question?
- **Enhance Relationships**
  - When was the last time you had an informal coffee or lunch with members of your team?
  - When was the last time you had an informal coffee or lunch with a colleague from another department or organization?

Whether you have a formal leadership title or are someone aspiring to be the best professional you can be within your field, the suggested questions can help to build rapport and trust. Once you have established this base within your working group, people will mirror your positive behaviors. Your positive collaborative behaviors will establish a model for your staff to merge individual strengths to recognize the unique perspective that each team member brings.

As Teilhard de Chardin envisioned, Emotionally Intelligent leaders work toward developing a collaborative workplace that embraces diversity and prioritizes inclusive teams made up of people who have different talents, opinions, and experiences.

This chapter introduced the importance of including staff in collaborative decision-making conversations and recognizing their contribution to the team efforts. The next chapter explores strategies to engage and motivate employees.

NOTES

1 Tippet, Krista. January 23, 2014. "Teilhard de Chardin's 'Planetary Mind' and Our Spiritual Evolution."
2 Dixon, Matthew, Ponomareff, Lisa, Turner, Scott, and DeLisi, Rick. "Kick-Ass Customer Service." (January–February 2017). *Harvard Business Review.* pp. 111–115.
3 Colonel Scott A. Jackson (personal interview, May 26, 2017).
4 Schein, Edgar. (2004). Organizational Culture and Leadership, 3rd Edition. (pp. 25–37). San Francisco: Jossey-Bass.
5 Detert, James R. and Burris, Ethan B. (January–February 2016). "Can Your Employees Really Speak Freely?" *Harvard Business Review.* Pp. 81–87.
6 U.S. Surgeon General's Office. (2022). *A Framework for Workplace Mental Health & Well Being.*
7 Gallup, Inc. (2023). *State of the Global Workplace 2023 Report: The Voice of the World's Employees.*
8 Gallup, Inc. (2023). *State of the Global Workplace 2023 Report: The Voice of the World's Employees.*
9 Cloud, Henry. (2013). Boundaries for Leaders. (pp. 42–43). New York, NY: Harper Business.
10 McGregor, Jena. (December 11, 2016). "For Lego CEO, rebuilding was no children's game," *The Washington Post.*

CHAPTER SUMMARY

Building Strengths

• Innovation cannot happen in a vacuum. Together, people build on each other's ideas to envision a reality that might never have been practiced before. Human empowerment drives technological advances, not vice versa.

- The most effective working groups are made up of people who represent a variety of roles to provide different perspectives and support functions.
- The culture of an organization is shaped by its public organizational image, the espoused values and business practices, and the unconscious organizational assumptions.
- Constructive conversations and regularly scheduled feedback sessions help people realize their work is appreciated and valued.
- Engaged and productive employees know they and their work matters.
- Successful matrix team leaders need to be able to recognize different communication and work styles, minimize competing objectives, and synchronize resource coordination and communications to maintain alignment of group and organizational goals.
- Leaders need to make sure that each team member takes on different task roles to leverage their capabilities, incorporate professional growth opportunities, and move the team toward the designated goal.
- Leaders need to be able to create conditions which will empower their team to pursue the needed action to achieve success.

6

Positive Workplaces

> Motivating factors imapct…
> Leaders provide guidance by…
> Values drive…

PATIENCE AND PERSEVERANCE

Building teams and collaborative conversations among diverse people takes time and can meander along a variety of paths before a resolution is achieved. An Emotionally Intelligent leader's role is to pay attention to the process to assure people stay motivated and on track. The challenge for leaders is being able to maintain the vision, meld the team strengths, and maintain positive energies. This is the part where working together to achieve a greater whole may seem like an unattainable endeavor. It requires a great deal of focus and energy. Leaders must constantly monitor all available feedback channels, be attuned to trending changes, mediate conflict, and enable adaptations to empower teams toward success. More often than not, leaders will need to draw on reserves of patience and diplomacy—multiple times each day—as they ensure that people stay motivated to achieve the desired goal.

LEADERSHIP—AN ANCIENT TALE

Helping people stay motivated by (1) focusing on what is important, (2) inhibiting activities that are not valuable, and (3) keeping everyone on track is a centuries old challenge for leaders. There is a wonderful story that

DOI: 10.1201/9781003520719-6

provides a simple example of motivational leadership during a very confusing moment in history. The ancient Babylonians conquered Jerusalem and destroyed the Holy Temple. The conquering generals ordered the Israelites to prepare for the journey to Babylonia where they were to be taken as slaves.

The Temple High Priest came upon several men pulling large stones from the rubble and queried their purpose. The men proudly reported they were planning to take the stones to Babylonia to rebuild the temple so they would have a place to pray while in exile. Instead of congratulating their efforts, the High Priest chastised them. He told the men the stones were much too heavy to drag during the arduous journey ahead; instead, they should be gathering food and clothing to support their families.

The men asked, "How will we pray without a temple?" The High Priest told them since they would be traveling for many weeks, an alternative place for prayer would be needed. In lieu of brick and mortar, he told them a sacred space would be created when a minimum of 10 men gathered to pray. Similar to our modern-day virtual teams, the Israelites were able to establish community norms and behaviors wherever their wanderings took them. Just as in ancient times, conference rooms and cubicles are not a requirement for people to be able to work together. An understanding that enables the convergence of cooperative human spirit is all that is needed to create a fully functioning community.

Even without the aid of modern-day leadership guidebooks, the High Priest demonstrated Emotionally Intelligent leadership when they (#1) focused the men's attention on the priority task of gathering survival essentials, (#2) stopped the men wasting energy trying to drag heavy stone pillars across the desert, and (#3) helped to keep them on track by providing an innovative solution to their concern that they would not be able to pray.

HUMAN AND ORGANIZATION NEED SATISFACTION

The Temple exile story demonstrates the leadership skill for helping people focus on the basics for survival before attacking a more complex goal. A more modern research model is Maslow's Hierarchy of Needs. During the mid-1940s, Dr. Abraham Maslow identified a five-level model which identifies the human needs that must be satisfied before "higher level" activities can be performed. Maslow's Hierarchy of human needs often is

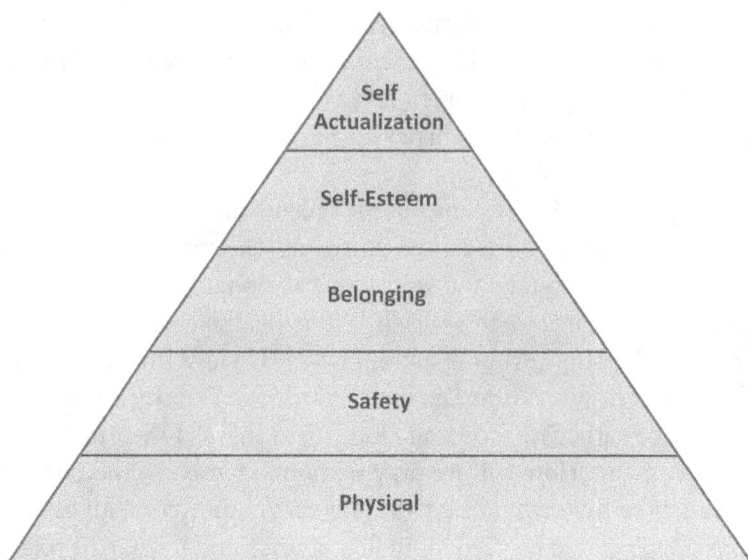

FIGURE 6.1
Hierarchy of organizational needs.

represented by a triangle or pyramid shape. The Hierarchy of Organization Needs model, illustrated by Figure 6.1, merges Maslow's five levels of individual well-being a person needs to achieve before they are able to perform to their potential.

Maslow's first level begins with basic human physiological needs: oxygen, food, water, sleep, etc. Once these are assured, individuals move their focus up to the safety, belonging, and self-esteem level. Only after basic survival, essential connections, and core self-esteem elements have been achieved by an individual can that person begin to work toward his/her optimal potential.

A person faces a similar hierarchy of needs before they can become a fully effective member of a new organization. Figure 6.2 identifies the Hierarchy of Organizational Needs and Communications as they parallel the traditional Maslow Pyramid. The first tier of the workplace pyramid begins with the on-boarding process that communicates the essential information a new employee needs to know when they begin working for the company. How and when do they get paid? Where are the restrooms? What are their assigned responsibilities? Where do they perform their work? Once a person is confident with the workplace essentials, the next step is to integrate them into their immediate workgroup.

FIGURE 6.2
Hierarchy of organizational needs and communication.[1]

The second tier of the workplace pyramid describes the purpose of the workgroup the new employee will be joining and how they will be contributing to achieving the departmental goal. What is the organization's purpose? What is the purpose for their assigned department? What is the new hire's role in the department? Why were they hired? What are their responsibilities?

The third team membership tier addresses how someone becomes a valued member of the team. How are new hires introduced? Is there a group on-boarding plan that includes resources and timelines for the new hire to become proficient in their position? Are people assigned an ambassador/buddy to help them meet team members and orient them to the cultural norms of the group?

The fourth tier addresses how the new hire learns to navigate the linkages between different departments in the organization. How does the work of their department coordinate with other departments? What information is needed by which groups? Who needs to be included in which procedural loop? Who can be called for assistance?

Much like Maslow's self-actualization level, the fifth tier aligns an individual's aspirations with the organization's vision. At this level, people proactively participate in a variety of formal/informal leadership roles. Professional development plans play an important role in helping people fully engage in an organization and support strong employee retention.

The following is a sample scenario using the Hierarchy of Organizational Needs and Communications as a guideline. When a merger or major organizational restructure is announced, it is important to focus on the essentials. People need to be assured that they will continue to have a job and their current salary will not be reduced. The next hurdle of concern for people is where they will fit within the new organization and the colleagues with whom they will be working. Once people are secure and confident of their place within the organization, they can then begin to establish linkages over which they channel their expertise and creativity to work with new and existing colleagues to help promote the new organizational mission.

CONSIDER AND DELIBERATE

Describe a situation when you felt as if the proverbial rug was pulled out from under you.

What was your initial reaction?

What was your second thought?

What was the process you used to work through this challenging situation?

What lessons were you able to take with you from this experience?

Reflecting back to a situation when you were not entirely comfortable will help you to recognize the needs of your team and develop motivational energies to help them through challenging transitions. You will be able to help your team and associated stakeholders perform to their best ability, because they know the survival essentials are handled and they trust the group of people with whom they are working.

THE ON-BOARDING PROCESS

An employee's experience during their first weeks with a company determines how they will engage. Beyond payroll forms, the on-boarding process is an opportunity for a new employee to learn how their work aligns with other employees to achieve organizational goals.

A Jobvite 2022 survey found that 32% of employees who left a job within the first 90 days cited company culture as the reason. The on-boarding process and welcome people receive from their colleagues reflect the company culture and set the tone for how people engage and work together. If employees do not connect with their colleagues and company culture during those first few days, they will begin their tenure disengaged and leave the company soon after their hire date.[2]

On-boarding offers newly hired employees an introduction to an organization's culture, the mission purpose, and resources they can use to assure their success. These procedures should be designed so that in addition to understanding their role and performance expectations, they have a clear understanding of how their work aligns with the organization mission.

Some best on-boarding practices include:

- Describe how their position contributes to the organization mission
- Clarify performance expectations

- Introduce new hires to people inside and outside their department
- Explain how employees stay in touch and communicate throughout the day
- Provide technology set-up support and training for on-site and remote work
- Pair new hires with a more tenured person

MOTIVATIONAL SATISFIERS AND DISSATISFIERS

Much research has been funded trying to understand what makes people do what they do. Some people self-motivate. Others need an external push. Managers may use a variety of positive or negative motivational tools to direct their teams toward a desired end. The most effective methods will depend on the motivator, the environment, and the person they are trying to encourage.

There is no simple answer when it comes to learning what motivates different individuals. Leading teams is similar to the experience of a parent when they discover that second and third children react differently to similar experiences than their first born. Even though they shared the same parents and grew up in the same household, each child in a family has their own physical and psychological makeup. It is natural they will have different needs and desires. When you bring people together in a workplace with different cultural and professional experiences, of course, not every motivational management technique will be successful for all situations. Emotionally Intelligent leaders pay attention to the people with whom they work to observe the different preferred motivators. This section introduces several theories that may help you understand and navigate different situations that you might encounter.

During the 1950s, Frederick Herzberg developed the Motivation Hygiene Theory which divides motivational practices for workers into two categories: Satisfiers and Dissatisfiers.

Tangible items such as salary increases and workgroup assignments that might be used to entice workers to continue with the organization are referenced as Dissatisfiers. These "carrots" when used to encourage dissatisfied workers seldom result in keeping the worker happy. The pay raise may keep the worker motivated for the short term, but at some point he or she will become unhappy again and leave.

Satisfiers are defined as actions associated with responsibility, growth, and recognition. These actions are less tangible, but assure happier, longer tenured workers. Satisfied workers appreciate salary increases. They continue working with the organization because they feel that they are important to the achievement of the organizational mission.

MOVING THE ELEPHANT—A MOTIVATIONAL METAPHOR

In the book *Switch: How to Change Things When Change Is Hard*, Dan and Chip Heath describe humans as being motivated by emotion and rational thought. They use the visual metaphor of a Rider on top of an Elephant to demonstrate how people are motivated by a variety of stimuli that balance the emotional and rational sides of the brain. The Rider is associated with the rational side of the brain and is most effectively motivated via clearly communicated explanations. The Elephant is associated with reactions described as emotional or "gut" reactions. The Elephant and the Rider provide counterpoints such that if a Rider does not have a clear vision of the route, he could lead the Elephant in circles. And, if the Elephant does not want to move in a certain direction, no amount of logical urging from the Rider will get the Elephant to move forward. There is a third element to this model the Heaths refer to as Shaping the Path. This concept provides helpful guides that make the journey easier by encouraging the Elephant and providing clarity to the Rider.

The Elephant-Rider-Path metaphor can be deployed even if you do not have supervisory power or a huge budget. This flexible methodology enables you to address different working personalities and help your group toward success. The simple checklist reminds you to:

1. Motivate the Elephant with a compelling reason.
2. Direct the Rider and establish clarity of purpose.
3. Shape the Path to assist the current situation.

This three-phase thought process allows you to adapt a group's motivation as the situation and requirements change. The one consistent consideration needs to be the end game that everyone is striving to reach together.[3]

CONSIDER AND DELIBERATE

Do you think your motivational needs tend more toward being a Rider or being an Elephant? Briefly describe a situation where you had not "bought into" the purpose until the leader ascribed to your rational or emotional motivational needs.

Does your motivational requirement (Rider vs Elephant) change depending on the situation? Can you briefly explain the circumstances?

Was there a time when you or the team leader needed to shape the path to help your team maintain their motivation?

Reflect on a time when changing circumstances caused you and your team to adjust your initial plan in order to achieve the designated goal. Who determined the change in method/direction was needed? How was the altered plan determined? How did the team react to the shift?

Maintaining both your own motivation and your team's motivation over the course of a long-term project can be a challenge. Changing circumstances can be frustrating for team members. The eventual completion of a project may not reflect the originally planned journey; however, your team will arrive together and have weathered a uniquely shared experience. Emotionally Intelligent leaders help team members continue to focus on the end goal and the value their efforts contribute toward the project success.

HIGH-IMPACT MOTIVATORS

Stakeholder management is one of the most important skills a 21st-century business leader can develop. Even the medical industry is putting more emphasis on interpersonal and patient and staff relationship skills as part of a physician's training program. Scott Magids and his research team explored "emotional motivators" that drive customer behavior. They discovered 10 high-impact motivators (Table 6.1) that successful retailers were able to "align themselves with emotions that drive their customers' most profitable behavior."[4]

TABLE 6.1

High-Impact Motivators That Significantly Affect Customer Value

I am inspired by a desire to:	Brands can leverage this motivator by helping customers:
Stand out from the crowd	Project a unique social identity; be seen as special
Have confidence in the future	Perceive the future as better than the past; have a positive mental picture of what's to come
Enjoy a sense of well-being	Feel that life measures up to expectations and that balance has been achieved; seek a stress-free state without conflicts or threats
Feel a sense of freedom	Act independently, without obligations or restrictions
Feel a sense of thrill	Experience visceral, overwhelming pleasure and excitement; participate in exciting, fun events
Feel a sense of belonging	Have an affiliation with people they relate to or aspire to be like; feel part of a group
Protect the environment	Sustain the belief that the environment is sacred; take action to improve their surroundings
Be the person I want to be	Fulfill a desire for ongoing self-improvement; live up to their ideal self-image
Feel secure	Believe that what they have today will be there tomorrow; pursue goals and dreams without worry
Succeed in life	Feel that they lead meaningful lives; find worth that goes beyond financial or socioeconomic measures

The 10 high-impact motivators that affect customer value continue to apply within today's workplace. Emotionally Intelligent leaders observe their reporting groups of people and map out a plan that enables them to motivate individuals so that they are able to work together to achieve the department/organizational goals.

ADVICE AND MOTIVATION

Once people are motivated to put a stake in the ground and become active team members, they begin to build collegial relationships as they learn how to work together. Demonstrating their strengths and leaning into other's talents requires various "water testing" methods. People may feel they are "making it up as they go along," because there are no concrete blueprints or standard operating procedures to reference.

Workplace pioneers involved with a new collaborative effort need to be comfortable with some level of uncertainty. They will look toward their managers, colleagues, and industry experts for advice. It is important to ask guiding questions and not give the easy answer. The encouragement received during these formal and informal advisory sessions has a strong impact on the seeker's continued motivation to pursue and explore.

A major role for collaborative team leaders is to provide support and guidance to help the teams stay on track. Have you ever gone to your team leader with a request for advice, but they didn't really provide you the guidance you were hoping to receive? David Garvin and Joshua Margolis summarize some of the challenges between advice seekers and advice providers in their article, "The Art of Giving and Receiving Advice." The basis for the article is the discovery that one of the most common sources of misunderstanding when someone seeks out guidance is the advice giver's role within the exchange.

As a leader, you will find yourself on both sides of being an advice seeker and an advice giver. All too often people seeking advice presume they already know the answer and are seeking validation. They then choose a like-minded advisor with similar experiences and viewpoints. These advisory reviews will produce a plan for which the weaknesses to the plan are reinforced and the strengths weaken. The result is akin to inbreeding. Similarly, advice seekers may not realize the breadth of advice they need and might overlook asking advice from someone who could offer valuable insights. Some of the most valuable advice an advisor can provide is the insight to help the Seeker find the best advisors who can provide critical breadth or depth for their consideration.

Garvin and Margolis organize guidance into four categories: discrete advice, counsel, coaching, and mentoring. Table 6.2 summarizes the guidance role the advice giver plays based on the type of information the seeker needs for that situation. Discrete advice is a query for specific information. More than likely, you are able to quickly respond to the Seeker's question or you will be able to forward them on to someone who will be able to help them. When requesting counsel, the seeker is usually looking for advice to help them create a framework to make a decision or take action. As the person providing counsel, you should avoid providing a specific prescription. The Seeker is looking for suggestions for a way forward as opposed to a specific suggestion. During your conversation, they may realize that one path will be better for them from another, but it should evolve from the Seeker's thought process, not yours.

When Seekers request coaching or mentoring type of advice, they are looking to develop an ongoing relationship. These two types of guidance often are interchanged; however, they represent two very different types of relationships. A Coach helps the seeker develop proficiency for a special skill, such as learning how to deliver a more effective presentation. Making a commitment to be a Mentor to someone is much more about helping the Seeker develop professional relationships for career advancement. Mentors may be able to introduce the Seeker to various people within their network for the purpose of gaining exposure.

TABLE 6.2

Advice Giver Roles Matrix

Type	Activities	Desired Outcomes
Discrete Advice	Exploring options for a single decision	Recommendations in favor of or against specific options
Counsel	Providing guidance on how to approach a complex or unfamiliar situation	A framework or process for understanding and navigating the situation
Coaching	Enhancing skills, self-awareness, and self-management	Task proficiency; personal and professional development
Mentoring	Providing opportunities, guidance, and protection to aid career success	A relationship dedicated to building and sustaining personal effectiveness and to career advancement

Independent of which type of advice someone is seeking, an advisor has the opportunity/responsibility to provide a constructive framework that the seeker may not have considered. The advisor could be a sounding board to offer a few insightful questions for the purpose of clarity, or help the seeker reshape their perspective by offering information that expands their breadth or depth of knowledge regarding the situation. If the Seeker wants to walk through a tentative plan, the advisor should review their assumptions and offer hypothetical situations to plan for possible consequences.[5]

CONSIDER AND DELIBERATE

How would you respond, if you asked someone for general guidance and the advisor directed a specific course of action for which you did not agree?

Describe a time when someone asked you a clarifying question that gave you some additional perspective. Were you grateful or grumpy during the interaction?

What standard clarifying questions do you ask people when you are trying to understand more about the question they are asking you?

How might you initiate a coaching session with someone who doesn't realize they need to improve a skill?

What information would you find beneficial from a mentor for your professional growth and development?

When people reach out to you to ask a specific or broader question, it is important to take a moment to check that you are providing the advice or counsel being asked. Some days are hugely busy and you may not be able to fully confirm that the information you provided was helpful. Don't be afraid to circle back to the person who asked your advice to verify that they have the information they need. If the Seeker has what they need, they will feel good that you respect them to be concerned. If you misunderstood what was needed, apologize that you couldn't provide your full attention and offer to discuss the issue now or at a scheduled time.

DIFFERENT PEOPLE NEED DIFFERENT MOTIVATIONS

Motivational techniques are not just for your direct reports. Depending on the situation, you may be called on to motivate a variety of people including folks who are your peers and people who are senior to you. Official and unofficial leaders need to use all of the tools they have to make sure that all involved in the project are able to focus on the goal and avoid any time-wasting actions. Feedback, both non-verbal and verbal, is even more important for the motivational process among colleagues. Your peers may have opinions and suggestions that will provide value to you. More often than not, you will need to adapt your motivational message for different audiences depending on their personalities and previous experiences.

The ritual Passover meal is a prime example of adapting your motivational message to different audiences. The story of Moses leading the Israelites out of Egypt where they had been enslaved for several generations to freedom is told every year when people gather for the Seder meal. Rituals involving symbolic foods and wine help participants to imagine that they are one of the slaves who are trying to escape to freedom and the lessons they learned along the way. The story and the progress of the holiday meal are orchestrated by a family member or friend who is encouraged to frame the story in different ways so all will be able to understand.

The guidelines for this segment of the holiday meal instruct the person who is leading the Seder (ritual meal) to adapt their explanation of the Passover story for four types of children(learners): the wise one, the ornery one, the simple one, and the child who does not even know how to ask a question. The wise child requires the leader to explain the story in great detail and nuance. The ornery one sees no relevance and considers the gathering a waste of time. For this child, the leader must work to help them understand their place in the story and how it relates to modern-day challenges. The simple one wants to learn, but has difficulty comprehending complex explanations. For this child, the leader needs to provide a simply worded explanation. And for the child who does not even know how to ask a question, the leader is expected to introduce the story and help them learn how to participate.

This metaphor can be used in almost every change situation as you try to facilitate new skills training and motivate team members to work together to achieve a common goal. There are people who love new challenges and want to know every detail. For these people, leaders may want to solicit their assistance to help smooth the transition. There are those people who will drag their feet and find the negative in anything that is new or different. Leaders will need to help these people understand the benefits the change will provide to them, the team, and the entire organization. There are people who are excited, but are nervous about significant change. For these people, leaders might want to move slowly—one step at a time. And for those who don't understand how the change will affect their work effort, leaders need to take a step back and explain how the tasks these people perform will fit into the larger vision.

MAPPING MOTIVATION TO VALUES

There are no simple answers when it comes to successfully motivating each individual working on a collaborative team. In addition to the normal diversity of personalities and cultural traits, working groups will consist of people representing different departments or partner organizations that support different workplace cultures.

Zachary Wong, an experienced project manager, shares a simple matrix (Table 6.3) to help people quickly map preferred motivation techniques for four general personality types in his book *Personal Effectiveness in Project Management.*

This is a great tool for comparison. It is important to remember that depending on the situation and their role, a person use when your team is forming and you are trying to make a relatively quick assessment of the structure of the team and the different motivational approaches you may need to take.[6]

In these instances, experience is very helpful as you observe and sort the various motivational requirements needed by your team members. Emotionally Intelligent leaders will not separate people into standard groupings according to their motivational profile. Use this knowledge to

TABLE 6.3

Personality/Motivational Technique Matrix

Personality	Characteristics	Motivations
Rational	Objective, Analytical, Technical, Logical	Being challenged Feeling recognized Having autonomy
Idealist	Amiable, Caring, Collaborative, Hopeful	Having a purpose Feeling respected and trusted Collaborating
Guardian	Organized, Diligent, Reliable, Compliant	Getting the job done Feeling needed Feeling appreciated
Artisan	Creative, Fun-Loving, Open, Self-expressive	Having freedom to act Feeling unique and potent Having admiration

speak with them one-on-one conversationally or during coaching situations. Your professional expectations for excellent work should not differ, only the context of your communication.

Essentially a leader is similar to a salesperson who sells a product such as an automobile to different customers who have different priorities. Your job is to figure out what is the primary motivation for different people. For example, if you are a car salesperson, you need to determine whether the potential customer is more concerned about safety, performance, style, or price. Once you identify their motivation to buy, you must shape your pitch accordingly. The goal is to sell a car. The method you choose to use may be slightly different for each potential customer. This is similar to Sitting Bull's strategy discussed in Chapter One when he addressed the specific strengths and interests of the individual Sioux chiefs' to motivate them to align with him and his plan to defeat Custer.

An example of how you might shape your motivational strategy for different team members can be taken from Sitting Bull's playbook (Chapter 1) and use flattery as a means of motivation. During an organizational meeting, discuss team member strengths or professional growth opportunities as you are making assignments. In the case of Rational Ruth, you might say, "Ruth, you did such a great job on the Configuration Management requirements on the last project, I would like you to take on …." For Idealistic Isaac who works best as part of a group, you might say, "Isaac, I appreciate you being able to uncover the essential feature in the procurement application. It would have been a disaster, if we had deleted it from the upgrade as we had originally planned. Would you take the lead coordinating with management to develop the end user training functions?" For Guardian Greg, you might say, "Greg, I'd really like you to monitor each team's progress to make sure we can stay on schedule. I appreciate your diplomatic abilities. I know I can count on you to establish trust with the team lead and you will be able to let me know when something unexpected is going to alter the schedule or budget by more than 5%. Lastly you might approach Artisan Amy, "Amy, I'd like to do something a bit different with our weekly status meetings. Will you help me develop some thoughts that will take traditional checklists to a different level?"

CONSIDER AND DELIBERATE

Reflect on a time when a manager demotivated you. Was it the specific task assigned to you, or was it how the task was assigned? Please explain.

Describe a time when you were assigned to a relatively unexciting task or project. Did you plod along or did you find a way to visualize the larger picture? How did management relate to you during this project?

If you were managing people who were assigned a less-than-exciting task or project, how might you motivate them to put forth an exemplary effort?

Many of us are self-motivated and take great pride in our individual work efforts. However, at the heart of exemplary group performance is an Emotionally Intelligent leader who is adept at using a variety of motivational techniques to bring out the best from each person. This chapter looked at a variety of motivational techniques to help people perform at their peak. The next chapter introduces strategies to minimize conflict and manage critical conversations before the performance of the group is negatively affected.

NOTES

1 ©2024 by Susan Schwartz of the River Birch Group. Reprinted with permission.
2 Venkatraman, Vivek. (April 3, 2023). Work culture Affecting Employee Retention? Retrieved February 17, 2024 from https://www.linkedin.com/pulse/work-culture-affecting-employee-retention-vivek-venkatraman/
3 Heath, Chip and Heath, Gary. (2010). Switch. (pp. 1–100). New York, NY: Broadway Books.
4 Magids, Scott, Zorfas, Alan, and Leeman, Daniel. (November 2015). The New Science of Customer Emotions: A Better Way to Drive Growth & Profitability. *Harvard Business Review*. p. 69.
5 Garvin, David A. and Margolis, Joshua D. (January–February 2015). "The Art of Giving & Receiving Advice." *Harvard Business Review*. pp. 61–71.
6 Wong, Zachary. (2013). *Personal Effectiveness in Project Management*. (pp. 32–33). Newton Square, PA: Project Management Institute.

CHAPTER SUMMARY

Focus and Motivation

- Leaders must constantly monitor all available feedback channels, be attuned to trending changes, and enable adaptations to empower teams toward success.
- Leaders are responsible for ensuring that employees are fully engaged from on-boarding with the organization throughout their tenure with the company.
- Leaders should use a variety of motivational techniques to bringing people together in a workplace with different cultural and professional experiences.

- Leaders need to adapt motivational techniques to maintain a team's focus on the end goal over the course of a long-term project.
- A major role for collaborative team leaders is to provide advice, support, and guidance to help teams stay on track.
- Recognize and encourage the unique strengths of group members.

7
Conflict and Critical Conversations

> Conversation empowers people to…
> Agreeability can cause…
> Complexity impacts conflict by …

Language can be a powerful tool for bringing people together. Collaborative conversations help people create innovative solutions by allowing them to build on each other's ideas. Previous chapters have illustrated positive examples of people listening, learning, and expanding their view of the world. This chapter offers suggestions for how Emotionally Intelligent leaders can use conversation to resolve conflict.

Pàdraig Ó Tuama, a theologian and poet, works with groups from around the world to resolve conflict using education, mediation, and dialogue. He has helped people across the globe, including Europe, Africa, and Australia, work through their hostilities using language to establish courtesy, inclusion, and generosity.

Ó Tuama reinforces the importance of words when he shares, "…we infuse words with a sense of who we are. And so therefore, you're not just saying a word; you're communicating something that feels like your soul. And it might even be your soul. So the choice of a particular word is really, really important." This is why people need to recognize the limits of their ability to understand a situation and the need for them to be able to reach out and ask other people to help them understand.[1]

DOI: 10.1201/9781003520719-7

In his book *In the Shelter*, Ó Tuama offers suggestions for creating calm within a troubled world. He included a favorite poem "Lost" by David Wagoner that contains the lines:

"Wherever you are is called Here,
And you must treat it as a powerful stranger"[2]

This is a powerful metaphor for handling the unplanned and unexpected that can cause rifts and conflict among colleagues and team members. Handling charged conversations is an essential skill for an Emotionally Intelligent leader. How do you treat someone who moves into your neighborhood, who joins your faith community, who joins your sports team, who is newly hired by your organization? Do you immediately exclude them from the "in crowd"? Or, do you welcome them and get to know them?

Similarly, how do you treat someone who disagrees with you and wants to discuss an alternative idea? Do you shut them down and slander them to others in the group? Or, do you explore their suggestion because it might make for a better solution? Most importantly, what do you do when you see people excluding others because they are new or disagree?

An Executive Vice-President of a large organization once told me, "Conflict is not bad. It is how you handle it that makes the difference." I was in my mid-20s when he shared that nugget of wisdom with me. My colleague and I reacted in an unprofessional manner during a meeting when we discovered one of his staff members had withheld information to discredit us. Visualize two young women in navy blue suits, stockings, and heels climbing across a conference table to throttle our false accuser. It was not a stellar moment. The two of us came to our senses before we were fully on top of the table. As my colleague and I were gathering our composure and offering apologies, Mr. D. (the Executive VP) looked us straight in the eye, and said, "Ladies, ladies, conflict is not bad, it is how you handle it that makes the difference." In that instant, he was letting us know that he realized we had been "set up" without blaming or embarrassing the person who did so.

We quickly resolved the problem and the meeting continued according to the agenda without any more surprise attacks from our nemesis. Mr. D. could have played into the situation the staff member had tried to set up. He could have chastised us. He could have demanded we be removed from the account. Instead, he chose to mentor us and provided invaluable counsel that we would take forward.

Navigating conflict is never smooth. The ability to guide teams from conflict to a creative solution using the generosity of language and listening is another trait that Emotionally Intelligent leaders develop. Pàdraig Ó Tuama established a retreat center named Corrymeela near Ballycastle in the west of Ireland. He tells a story about the name people originally thought meant "hill of harmony." A few years after opening someone better versed in old Irish etymology (sic) interpreted Corrymeela as "place of lumpy crossings."[3] What better word describes the process of working through conflict than "lumpy crossings"? Conflict does not come with directions. Rarely is one conflict ever handled in the same manner as another. It takes an experienced leader to guide the team across the various 'lumpy crossings' on the way to resolution.

CONSIDER AND DELIBERATE

Reflect on a recent conflict that took place within your professional or community environment. What action ignited the conflict?

Was the conflict a simple situation to resolve or was it a "lumpy crossing"?

Briefly describe "the wrong" that each party felt.

Describe the actual challenge that the eventual resolution resolved.

What actions were taken from the incident that initiated the resolution process to the end solution?

Sometimes, people postpone confrontation because they don't want to cause a scene or think the infraction is not worth making a fuss about. The challenge for leaders is to help their team to understand a courteous conversation that resolves a small problem goes a long way toward heading off an extreme conflict that may involve many people and take much time away from daily work activities.

CRUCIAL CONVERSATIONS

Kerry Patterson and his team of researchers developed the concept of crucial conversations as a means to maintain courteous dialogue when you are approached to address a challenging situation immediately, but are unprepared to do so. A crucial conversation usually occurs spontaneously during very public moments. An audience is always present to see your discomfort as you try to respond to the unexpected query. The topic is high risk because both of you feel very strongly about your opinions and the consequences of how you respond can have long-term effects.

Whether the situation is professional or personal, the timing and possibility of an explosive response is the foremost driver to determine how you respond. Have you ever had someone ask you a question about a project which wasn't going well, in front of the boss? Or, has someone angrily approached you when you were in the middle of a conversation in the office break room? People's default response to these types of queries either is to avoid conflict by saying nothing or to say something they might regret. Neither of these silent or violent reactions is a constructive means for handling conflict. The third option is to manage the situation with skill and grace.

Many times people do not realize their natural reactions until after the situation has occurred. The key to having a strong leader-like response at the ready is to practice your reaction to difficult situations before they happen. Table 7.1 offers several common reactions to challenging situations. Read through each of the reactions to a challenging situation. If you have responded using one of these methods, place a check in the column labeled "I Do This." In the third column labeled "Behavior," identify the type of behavior as: avoidance, sarcasm, change topic, coercion, dismissive, or attack.

When you are confronted by a crucial situation, the only person you can control is yourself. The person initiating the query might present a sense of urgency; however, there is no rule that states you must respond immediately to the query. A simple statement such as, "I appreciate your concern,

TABLE 7.1

Reactions to Challenging Situations Comparison Table

I Do This	Challenging Situation Reaction	Behavior
	I delay returning texts, emails, or phone calls because I don't want to deal with the issue. If I ignore the person they will go away.	
	I am a very direct person and let people know when I think their ideas are stupid and will never succeed.	
	I try to counter harsh feedback with a positive comment or a self-deprecating joke.	
	I don't give harsh feedback when I don't want to deal with the consequences.	
	I tend to make absolute statements (e.g. everyone knows…, it's obvious to anyone…) when I believe my idea is a better way to handle a situation than anyone other under discussion.	
	I try to make my point in an even tone, but sometimes the other person makes me feel so disrespected, I explode and say the wrong thing which only makes me appear weaker.	
	I suddenly remember an urgent appointment when someone brings up a topic I do not want to discuss.	
	I find responding with sarcasm to ideas I don't think will work softens the blow to the other person.	
	I try to work through the conflict with others so we can work together to find out the real cause of the problem.	
	I will suggest a cooling off break or reschedule the discussion when the people get caught up blaming others and stop looking for solutions.	

let's block out some time tomorrow so that we can give the situation the full attention it deserves," defuses the situation, respects the person trying to bully your response, and offers you time to gather relevant information. Even if you are not able to postpone the crucial conversation, request a moment to gather your thoughts and focus on the essential priority by verifying your goals[4]:

1. For yourself
2. For your team including any related stakeholders
3. For the relationship you share with the person confronting you

STABILIZING CRUCIAL MOMENTS

Emotionally Intelligent leaders will not allow themselves to be bullied by an unexpected situation they are not immediately prepared to handle. They will stabilize an emotionally charged situation and arrange to schedule the discussion when all relevant information can be brought into the dialogue.

The secret to remaining calm during an emotionally charged moment is to remember it is the adrenaline, not necessarily the actual situation, which is creating the charged stressful moments. Kerry Patterson and his research team studied several key performance indicators (KPIs) at a variety of companies before and after their employees had gone through training and become skilled at crucial conversations. They discovered measurable performance and financial results could be attributed to these new skills. A few examples of these measurable results enabled staff to[5]:

- Adjust budgets five times faster in response to financial downturns
- Save over $1,500 and eight hours of employee time for each crucial conversation engaged
- Increase effectiveness of virtual teams which is directly attributed to increases in trust and reduced time to complete work tasks

A common factor among the official and unofficial leaders who were able to build relationships, increase productivity, and demonstrate positive financial results were present in the moment. They stepped back from their ego and any self-serving emotions and focused on the immediate organizational needs to be met. They used simple negotiation and conversation tools to stabilize the potentially crucial moment.

The power of an "And" statement enables people to create a mutual goal while avoiding a negative situation. An example of this type of mutual goal is, "The project plan needs to be completed within 60 days and not exceed $100,000." Since each party (e.g. sales and finance) participates in framing the goal, they share ownership and a mutual stake in the creative process to explore solutions to achieve success. A corollary to the mutual "And" is the contrasting "And" statement that juxtaposes two core points of view: "I don't want _____ to happen and I do want _____ to happen. An example of a contrasting "And" statement is "We need to figure out a solution that will enable us to finish the project by the end of month and continue staffing the telephone support lines."

Dr. Anthony Suchman made a career out of researching how to get conversations that are starting to spiral out of control back on track. His research identified two channels over which all workplace conversations travel: the task channel and the relationship channel. He discovered that when task-focused disagreements spill over into the parallel relationship channel, emotions escalate and civil conversation constraints begin to break down. This breakdown is explained by neurological science. When a conversation appears to be headed toward disagreement, one or both parties activate their fear response. The hypothalamus, located in the front portion of the brain, triggers a fight-or-flight response which focuses attention toward survival needs. This involuntary fear response stops a person's capacity to think creatively.

Unfortunately, alternative ideas brought forward for discussion can be erroneously interpreted as a personal attack because the person who offered the original idea perceives the feedback as a personal attack. Their primal response wants to know why you don't like them, because you don't like their idea. Dr. Suchman suggests a series of conversational statements which can navigate the conversation back toward separate task and relationship channels. These collaborative relationship-building value statements referenced by the acronym PEARLS are illustrated in Table 7.2.[6]

For example, you might be working with someone who does not want to consider any other solution except the one they have developed. The comments identified in Table 7.2 are prompts that can help you build a more positive relationship and redirect constructive energies to the task focus. It is possible that the other person is afraid that you will not consider their concern. By telling them you want to work with them will let

TABLE 7.2

PEARLS Collaborative Value Statements

	PEARLS Collaborative Value Statements
Collaborative Value	**Suggested Statement Sample**
Partnership	I really want to work with you to solve this problem
Empathy	I hear your concern
Acknowledgment	I can see you have put a lot of time and effort into this
Respect	I appreciate your expertise in this area
Legitimation	I agree, there are several aspects that should be considered
Support	I want to help you successfully resolve this challenge

Source: Friedman (2016).

them know your goal is to create a joint partnering conversation. Perhaps they began working on a solution and are worried that you will want to "start fresh" and discard their hard work. Even if you totally disagree with their approach, focus on building the relationship by acknowledging their efforts. These brief comments can foster productive collaborative conversations.

DRIVING OFF TO ABILENE

Sometimes in an effort to build an important relationship, people can be too agreeable and take action that no one actually wants to pursue. They agree because they think it was important to the other person with whom they wanted to build a relationship. Jerry B. Harvey, author of *The Abilene Paradox: The Management of Agreement,* classifies this behavior as the "inability to manage agreement" since there is no conflict present to manage. Harvey recognized this phenomenon of people taking action on what they believe others want as opposed to the actual preferences of the people involved while visiting his in-laws in West Texas as a newlywed during the early 1950s.

Imagine a hot dusty summer afternoon on a West Texas cattle ranch. The temperature is 104° Fahrenheit and there is no air conditioning. Harvey, his wife, and her parents were sitting on the screen porch lazily sipping cold drinks. Wanting to entertain his guests, his father-in-law announced they should take a 40-minute drive to the nearest town, Abilene, for a steak dinner at his favorite restaurant. Harvey's wife responded, "Daddy what a wonderful idea!" Harvey could not imagine anything worse than a 40-minute drive in a car with no air conditioning through a dust storm for a heavy West Texas steak dinner. He didn't want to disagree with his wife and looked toward his mother-in-law to be the voice of reason and disagree. Mom simply agreed that it was too hot to cook. The group took the hot, dusty 40-minute ride, ate a large dinner, and drove home through the hot, dusty evening. They returned to the screened porch, where his father-in-law complained loudly about how badly he felt after the heavy meal and the hot dusty drive home. His mother-in-law said she only agreed to go because she thought everyone else wanted to go. Harvey's wife said she only agreed because she thought her daddy wanted to go so very much. His father-in-law said he only suggested it because he wanted to make sure his daughter and son-in-law enjoyed their visit. As it turned out, each of them would have been very happy spending the evening visiting on the screen porch and eating a light snack.[7]

"Driving off to Abilene" is not the same as avoiding a crucial conversation in which people are fully aware of the other person's point of view, but don't want to deal with a potentially explosive situation. In an Abilene-like situation, the individuals assume a collective reality that is not true. In being too agreeable, the people involved look toward the easiest path forward and do not take the time to validate the data or notice non-verbal cues.

When groups "Drive off to Abilene," their willingness to accept inaccurate information is a sure way for counterproductive results to be generated. Instead of building a strong relationship, the end result is that people become frustrated and often begin to blame each other as they try to identify the culprit who is responsible for the lack of communication and understanding.

CONSIDER AND DELIBERATE

Describe a time when you avoided a conflict situation. What were your reasons for not wanting to address the situation?

Describe a time when you were frustrated with how a colleague handled a difficult situation.

Looking forward, how might you use a crucial conversation technique to handle a similar situation differently?

Describe a time when you were with a group of people who made a decision to do something and later discovered no one actually wanted to participate but went along because they thought everyone else wanted to participate.

How did you feel when you discovered no one wanted to participate but went along because they thought everyone else wanted to pursue the activity?

Moving forward, what will you do when you find yourself in a situation where you are going along with what you believe to be a majority preference?

When people are starting to find that they are heading toward "Abilene," Emotionally Intelligent leaders help these teams create safe environments where they can discuss potential problems and share different opinions so that the decision becomes a group decision and an assumption of that people think others want to happen.

CREATING SAFE CONVERSATION SPACES

Leaders may find themselves working against established organizational norms when they begin to create an environment that encourages group members and stakeholders to participate in honest, open conversations that allow for hard topics to come to the forefront without setting off danger alarms.

Organization norms are established over the course of time based on a complicated matrix of actions and omissions. These spoken and unspoken norms were never written as official policy; however, they were reinforced by the premise "that is the way we do things here." Fear of potential repercussions inhibits people from questioning people who they believe are more experienced or possess greater authority. Add the complexity of multiple structures across a matrix organization and it is easy to see how often the very best intentions can be misinterpreted.

Mark Kramer and Marc Pfitzer work with governments and NGOs to help people create shared value to promote social change. They are familiar with the various patterns where individuals trying to pursue a joint vision find themselves in a muddle because they misinterpreted each other's actions. Kramer and Pfitzer have successfully helped to coordinate the efforts of government, business, and philanthropic organizations to work together to coordinate their efforts and develop a solution that emphasizes a successful collective community impact. Their techniques can be applied within a complex, matrix organization to create a safe shared space to pursue conversation. Successful collective impact efforts are based on five core elements:

- Common agenda
- Shared measurement system
- Mutually reinforcing activities
- Constant communication
- Dedicated "backbone" support

The common agenda is described as a shared vision for change and joint approach that is collaboratively discussed and mutually agreed upon by all involved parties. Depending on the complexity of the populations involved, the initial phase to reach a common agenda can take several months to address the full spectrum of issues and policies.

The shared measurement system should consist of a few key performance indicators by which people can measure their progress. The next element for success recognizes that each member of the collaborative group has a different set of skills and talents. The mutually reinforcing activities element recognizes that each person will contribute toward the greater whole based on their strengths, capabilities, and resources.

It is very easy for a diverse group of people who are used to working within separate organizations to isolate themselves and their assigned tasks from the rest of the collaborative group. Constant informal and structured communications are essential for people to maintain the synchronous rhythms that help to establish connections among coordinating organizations. The final essential element of dedicated "backbone" support is a separate independent staff that represents the interests of all organizational parties. The "backbone" is a group of people who are dedicated to the success of the initiative. They provide vision, supporting policies, shared measurement practices, and resource mobilization.[8]

Once an organization has a shared vision and an endorsement to move forward, the leaders charged with launching change within the organization need to pay attention to how they can create a new system that will encourage new behaviors and reward performance parameters. Whether the organization is categorized as a small-to-medium or enterprise conglomerate, Emotionally Intelligent leaders will juggle different types of demands when they work across a variety of departmental structures and management styles to help people adapt and grow to realize the new vision.

A leadership method that works within one type of organizational situation will not necessarily work across every situation. Leaders need to develop a variety of tools to respond appropriately to the situation at hand. David Snowden and Mary Boone developed a framework to recognize and appropriately address the complexities of an organization structure. The Cynefin (pronounced ku-*nev*-in) framework enables executives to rapidly assess, recognize and respond to real world situations. Snowden and Boone have worked with a variety of complex organizations across private industries and government agencies to validate the effectiveness of the Cynefin framework.

The Cynefin framework is based on four types of organization environments: Simple, Complicated, Complex, and Chaotic. Table 7.3 illustrates this framework by identifying the characteristic traits for each environment and the role a leader should play within this type of environment. Common organizational danger signals are identified for each environment along with a suggested response to help resolve or mitigate the challenging situation. A fifth category labeled "Disorder" represents a jumbled conglomeration of all four environments. The authors suggest people address a Disorderly environment head-on by separating out structural entities and matching each structural element to whichever of the four basic organization environments best describes the situation.[9]

A *Simple* environment is classified as an organization for which the executive management makes decisions based on facts derived from consistent operational patterns. The variables and the associated operational ranges are known entities. Leaders within these organizations focus on traditional management best practices and procedures. When staff begins to exhibit complacent attitudes, minimize operational problems, and hold onto rigid belief systems, leaders need to take action to reverse the organizational trend. The best response to jump-start people who you feel are becoming too complacent and accepting of the status quo is to challenge their current beliefs and best practices. Play devil's advocate and push them to view the situation from another perspective and to push them to reach beyond their comfort level.

A *Complicated* environment challenges executive management because every decision has several potential solutions. Organizational decisions are

TABLE 7.3

The Cynefin Framework

Environment	Organization Characteristics	Leader's Role	Danger Signals	Needed Response
Simple	Fact-based Management Consistent Patterns Known Knowns	Direct Delegation Best Practices Proper Procedures	Complacency Oversimplification of Problems Rigidity	Challenge Beliefs Link Into Process Recognize Best Practice Limits
Complicated	Diagnostics Required Multiple Possible Answers Known Unknowns	Situation Analysis Expert Advice Conflict Assessment	Overconfidence Narrow Focus Analysis Paralysis	Challenge Expert Opinions Think Outside Box Involve Stakeholders
Complex	Creative Approach Needed Unpredictability Unknown Unknowns	Purposeful Communications Idea Generation Create Safe Spaces	Command and Control Narrow Focus Resolution Urgency	Delegate Solution Tasks Encourage Brainstorming Reflection
Chaotic	No Cause Effect Urgent Decisions Unknowables	Order and Alignment Solution Seeking Communication	Tight Controls Risk Aversion No Forward Progress	Parallel Teams Devil's Advocate Separate Tasks

based on a series of analytical procedures that prioritizes risks associated with all of the possible consequences that could result from the selection of one of the solutions based on the known unknown variable. Leaders within a *Complicated* organization environment are dependent on advice from subject matter experts (SMEs); however, they need to practice sound situational analysis to be able to logically assess conflicting expert opinions. Leaders need to watch out when recommendations are based on a very narrow focus and staff members become overconfident in their ability to resolve the situation. In these instances, leaders need to help staff members expand their perspective and thought process. Bringing knowledgeable stakeholders into these conversations may be an excellent means to challenge team experts to try alternate methodologies that might stimulate some innovative solutions.

A *Complex* environment challenges executive management based on the total unpredictability of the situation. Individuals who prefer traditional management styles will not survive within this environment because all decision variables are unknown. Leaders within this type of environment need to help employees develop a culture that supports a creative approach to solution analysis and decision-making. Leaders must render purposeful communications. If they are not careful, every casual remark will be taken to represent a change in direction.

On the other hand, innovation is the foundation for success within *Complex* organizations and people look to leaders to establish safe places where staff members are encouraged to generate ideas. The danger signs for dysfunction within this environment are behaviors that inhibit creative conversations. Teams and individuals may take on a command and control demeanor which can limit the creative solutions. As people jockey for command & control positions, there is a tendency for every problem and its resolution to be an absolutely urgent priority. Every decision becomes an urgent fire drill. In this situation where power games are commandeering the creative process, leaders need to step in and organize the team into smaller groups that will address different aspects of the solution.

Group guidelines would encourage innovative solutions while defining the project scope and align the different group efforts when all of the elements are connected together. Managing urgencies can be a difficult challenge to balance. Once a leader realizes that there is not an immediate fire to put out, they can ask the team questions to encourage them to reflect on the challenge and realize in the calm after the initial storm a constructive solution and lessons that can be taken forward to avoid the situation in the future.

A *Chaotic* environment is just that—chaos. The executive management team is challenged because there is no logic to any decision within the organization and they cannot depend on any type of precedent to help guide them. People need leaders to establish some level of order and help them to align their work activities with the organization's mission.

Leaders within *Chaotic* environments are constantly troubleshooting as they try to establish a structure. Communication is a leader's key to success in these situations. It is human nature, when faced with chaos, for leaders to try to organize their little piece of the world; however, if leaders find their staff beginning to become risk averse, set tight controls, and have several excuses to explain why they are not meeting commitments, they need to take action. One suggestion to help leaders get their teams back on track in a *Chaotic* environment is to separate the work projects into achievable tasks and assign people to work in parallel teams with regularly scheduled meetings to update each group's progress and challenges.

CONSIDER AND DELIBERATE

Which of the Cynefin environments summarized in Table 7.3 describes your current organization? Provide a brief example to explain your selection.

How do you or your organizational leadership align with the description of the leader's role within the organization? What other leadership traits do you recognize as being helpful within your organization at this time?

As an organization develops in size and function, there is a natural flow from a Simple to a Complicated environment. What types of professional development activity would you recommend for executives who are involved in the growth process?

Which of the four workplace environments identified in Table 7.3 do you think you would find most rewarding to work within? Why?

The Cynefin framework demonstrates that not all leadership skills are transferable from one situation to another. Emotionally Intelligent leaders need to be alert to the needs of a situation and be able to determine whether they should bring in someone with the necessary expertise or take the identified gap as a professional development skills training opportunity.

ACCOUNTABILITY AND CONVERSATIONS

David Ignatius wrote an opinion article for The Washington Post which began with an anecdote about a former Central Intelligence Agency director visiting a top secret facility. During his visit, the staff gave him a T-shirt printed with the words, "Admit Nothing, Deny Everything, Make Counter Accusations."[10] The sentiment respectfully poked fun at some possibly well-earned stereotypes that various intelligence operatives may have earned over the years; however, how many of us have worked for managers who have done just that?

This is a good time to revisit the practice of trust among functional teams as described by Brené Brown which was discussed in Chapter 1. She describes functional teams as groups who respond to difficult situations by "turning toward each other" as opposed to "turning on each other."[11] Dysfunctional leaders encourage teams to blame each other when they model poor behaviors by refusing to admit they had a part in causing a problem, much less take ownership to resolve it. Often these leaders will select and punish someone they want to be responsible.

Accountability is demonstrated when a person takes responsibility for the cause and resolution of the problem. People do not need to be the designated leader to be accountable for a situation. Accountability can be contagious. When someone demonstrates the courage and mindset of accountability, others will follow their lead.

When Kerry Patterson and his research team were pursuing follow-up studies for their work with crucial conversations, they discovered people could learn how to address a difficult situation, but they could not always convince people to alter their behaviors. There will always be people who believe rules are meant for other people. Pursuing this line of inquiry, they discovered that 93% of the people they polled worked with a widely-recognized challenging type of person, but people were afraid to address the problem. They were reluctant to bring up behaviors which bent the rules or went against the norms because they feared the consequences. Patterson's team coined this phenomenon as an epidemic of silence. People were torn between what they thought were their only choices: say nothing and enable the poor behavior or potentially create a problem for themselves by calling out the bad behavior and facing negative consequences.

Broken commitments are one of the most significant behaviors people want to address when people discuss the need for accountability. Patterson's research team discovered that more than 70% of project managers were substantially behind schedule and over budget because no one spoke up when the executives created unattainable deadlines and budget forecasts. As the researchers queried the project managers being polled to discover how they found themselves in this dire situation, many of them replied that no one spoke up when the executive management established unattainable milestones. Those who did speak up were told there was no choice—make it happen. Rarely, did the executives who determined the schedule and budget accept responsibility when the milestones were missed.

Patterson's team also discovered when cross-functional teams were jointly working on a project, team members rarely would own up to problems that could affect the entire team. Colleagues working within a cross-functional group brought a difficult challenge to the project manager to discuss and resolve less than 20% of the time. This means more than 80%

of the time, milestones were missed because no one communicated that project indicators were off track.[12]

CONSIDER AND DELIBERATE

Describe a time when you did not own a mistake you made. What consequences caused you to defer your accountability?

Given the benefit of hindsight, how would you behave differently if you found yourself in a similar situation today?

Describe a time when someone denied accountability and deftly maneuvered you and your team into the position of responsibility. How did you feel?

How did you handle the situation? Given the benefit of hindsight, how would you handle the situation differently today?

It takes great courage to sustain an accountability mindset for yourself and your team when a situation is out of your span of control. Sometimes it may seem easier to look the other way and dust up any evidence since it was someone else's decision. Emotionally Intelligent leaders take on the challenge of guiding people to take ownership of a difficult situation and collaborate as a group to create a successful outcome.

TRAVELING TOWARD ACCOUNTABILITY

Patterson and his team identified a set of *Crucial Accountability* procedures to help people learn how to guide a constructive conversation that encourages people to assume accountability. Similar to a *Crucial Conversation*, the first 30 seconds is essential. This brief moment will determine whether your conversation will be collaborative or combative. In fact, his team refers to this moment as the "hazardous half-minute."

Before you begin the discussion, it is essential to have a plan. Identify and prioritize the behaviors you want to address. Review the potential consequences for each potential behavior. Then determine the behaviors you would like to occur from the conversation and the behaviors you do not want to continue as an outcome for the conversation. Finally, review what you do and don't want for yourself, others, and the relationship. The next series of steps vary slightly depending on the situation. They involve gathering facts, framing your story, and creating a conversation that will close the expectations gap.[13]

The Accountability Action model[14] illustrated in Figure 7.1 expands on the four-step Path to Action model developed by Patterson's team. The first step is to assure you have gathered all of the available facts. Sometimes appearances can be deceiving. There is an adage, "each has less than one half of 100% of the truth," which means as hard as we try to gather facts and look through multiple lenses, we can still miss a key point to the story.

The next phase focuses on a leader's listening and observation skills. There is a strong chance that while you believe someone is not taking ownership for their actions, the person in question understands their role and the associated expectations differently. To their mind, they are performing well. Another person may be working through a personal crisis and have not told anyone about the external difficulties they are trying to juggle. Sometimes, a person may not realize the consequences an action might have on the rest of the organization. And unfortunately, someone might be trying to blame someone else for their mistake.

Emotionally Intelligent leaders give people the benefit of the doubt, and gather the facts that relate to the situation initiated by poor performance and missed milestones. They begin conversations in a safe space. Do not make this an inquisition. Begin with open-ended questions regarding the status of the project. You can mention you've noticed they might have something

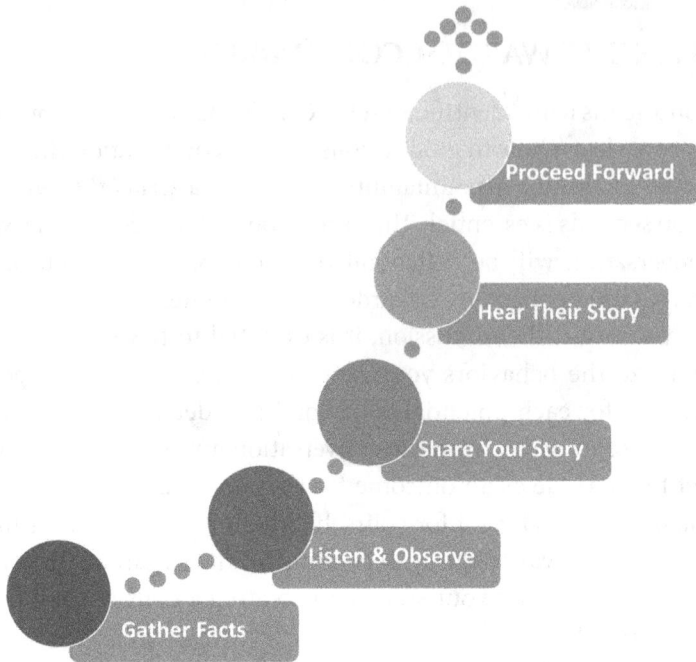

FIGURE 7.1
Accountability action model.

on their mind. This is a conversation, continue to gather data by listening to what they are saying and not saying. Watch their body language.

Once you have an understanding of their perspective of the situation that concerns you, move on to the third phase. Explain that you perceive the situation differently. Use the facts you have gathered to back up the scenario you are shaping during this conversation. Maintain an even tone as you point out the gaps where your expectations do not align with theirs. It is helpful to write your concerns down prior to this conversation so that you won't forget an important point or lose your train of thought in case the person you are meeting with gets emotional or insists on defending their view of the role. The most important point to remember is to reassure them that your priority is for the project and all people working with the project team to be successful. You will be honest with your team and hope they can be honest with you regarding challenges that can adversely affect the project.

The fourth phase is important because when the person with whom you are speaking becomes enlightened by the reality they may not have understood; they will begin to share information that can be leveraged for a resolution that will allow both of you and the rest of the team to move forward successfully. Do not roll your eyes when you perceive they are offering one more round of excuses, listen from your heart. Listen to what they are sharing and respond with questions that will enable them to take ownership of the situation. Sometimes people don't realize they have the authority to make decisions or initiate certain actions. They might not have been allowed to make these types of judgments as part of their prior experiences. They could be afraid of incurring management's wrath. It might be automatic for you to take action and do what you believe is needed to make the milestone happen; however, sometimes, people need permission.

The fifth and final phase of an accountability action conversation has the potential to make a constructive change in your organization. The agreement of what actions or tasks may vary according to the situations and people involved. The summation of your conversation should be positive as you provide the person feedback that you trust their judgment and provide them permission to which decisions they should make and which decisions should be brought to you. You might learn that certain aspects of the project were not going as planned and people were afraid to bring it to your attention. Or you might learn that the current job assignment is not a good fit, and your conversation may turn to a discussion of next steps to help this person find a more successful path.

CONSIDER AND DELIBERATE

Reflect on a situation for which you did not have the appropriate experience. How did you balance your learning curve and accountability for the task completion?

Was the experience you described above successful? Was there a key success factor you can attribute to a positive experience? If the experience was not successful, in hindsight, how could you have handled the situation differently?

Describe a situation when you needed to help a new person gain expertise quickly in order for a task to complete. What was your role: a colleague, a supervisor, or a reporting team member?

Was the situation a positive or negative experience? If positive, what about the scenario that made it successful? If it was negative, what were the key factors that caused a downfall? How might you handle the situation differently, if given a similar scenario today?

Given the benefit of hindsight, how would you behave differently, if you found yourself in a similar situation today?

By encouraging continual, factual communication among everyone involved with a situation, Emotionally Intelligent leaders are able to monitor project status and requirements to assure people have the necessary skills and resources to achieve success. Being accountable does not mean being all-knowing. Accountability is about addressing issues as they arise and working with your team to determine the most appropriate solution for the challenge at hand. Conflict will occur because people will bring different perspectives and priorities; however, by maintaining constructive conversation techniques with a focus on shared goals, Emotionally Intelligent leaders will maximize the opportunity for innovation and productivity improvements.

This chapter explored strategies to use constructive conversation techniques to mitigate conflict. The next chapter continues this theme to manage potential conflict that accompanies the uncertainty of change.

NOTES

1 Tippett, Krista. On Being. (March 2, 2017). "Belonging Creates and Undoes Us Both."
2 Tippett, Krista. On Being. (March 2, 2017). "Belonging Creates and Undoes Us Both."
3 Tippett, Krista. On Being. (March 2, 2017). "Belonging Creates and Undoes Us Both."
4 Patterson, Kerry, Grenny, Joseph, McMillan, Switzler, Al. (2012). *Crucial Conversation, 2nd Edition*. (pp. 1–49). New York, NY: McGraw Hill.
5 Patterson, Kerry, Grenny, Joseph, McMillan, Switzler, Al. (2012) *Crucial Conversation, 2nd Edition*. (pp. 111–114). New York, NY: McGraw Hill.
6 Friedman, Ron. (Fall 2016). "Defusing an Emotionally Charged Conversation with a Colleague." (pp. 24–25). *Harvard Business Review on Point*.
7 Harvey, Jerry, (Summer 1988). *Organization Dynamics*. (pp. 17–43). New York, NY: The American Management Association.
8 Kramer, Mark and Pfitzer, Marc. (October 2016). "The Ecosystem of Shared Value." (pp. 81–89). *The Harvard Business Review*.
9 Snowden, David J. and Boone, Mary E. (Winter 2015). *A Leader's Framework for Decision Making*. (pp. 71–78). *Harvard Business Review on Point*.
10 Ignatius David. (April 5, 2017). "Trump's shell game on Russia." *The Washington Post*. (p. A17).
11 Brown, Brené. (2012). *Daring Greatly*. (p. 101). New York, NY: Avery.
12 Patterson, Kerry, Grenny, Joseph, McMillan, Switzler, Al. (2013). *Crucial Accountability, Second Edition*. (pp. 1–14) New York, NY: McGraw Hill.
13 Patterson, Kerry, Grenny, Joseph, McMillan, Switzler, Al. (2013). *Crucial Accountability, Second Edition*. (pp. 149–198). New York, NY: McGraw Hill.
14 ©2017 by Susan Schwartz of the River Birch Group. Reprinted with permission.

CHAPTER SUMMARY

Conflict and Critical Conversations

- Language is a powerful tool for bringing people together. Collaborative conversations have the power to help people create innovative solutions as they build on each other's ideas.
- Crucial conversations are high-risk situations where the purpose of the instigator is to catch you off guard to either purposely make you look foolish publicly or elicit an automatic yes answer to their request.
- Strong leaders stabilize crucial moments by remaining calm and using stabilizing techniques to diffuse the emotionally charged moment and create a safe space to constructively discuss the issue.
- "Driving off to Abilene" describes a situation in which people are unable to work toward an agreement because no one actually knows anyone else's preference and everyone involved is making decisions based on assumptions and not facts.
- Safe conversational spaces enable people to explore new ideas without fear of repercussions.
- Accountability is one of the traits of successful teams because all members take responsibility for the cause and resolution of challenges that affect the group and the achievement of shared goals.

8

Growth and Uncertainty

Adaptation drives ...
Failure helps...
Uncertainty provides...

Throughout history many leaders have been hesitant to step forward to lead change. Sometimes it is because they are fearful as in the case of Steve Wozniak. He admitted not wanting to start a company because he was afraid. It took a concerted effort by Steve Jobs, friends, and his parents before he gained the confidence to leave steady employment and put his full energies into creating Apple Computer. Michelangelo refused the Pope's request to paint the ceiling of the Sistine Chapel for two years because he believed he did not have the talent needed to do justice to such an overwhelming commission.[1]

How do people know when to say "yes" to an overwhelming challenge? Sometimes other people may see your potential and push you forward. Sometimes everyone else in the group steps back leaving you to rise to the occasion. Other times you choose to look at a situation with fresh eyes to see what you can contribute.

Have you ever found yourself in a situation where it turned out to be more complex than you or your manager had anticipated? As you took that deep breath and began to work through the various challenges, I bet at the end of the day you learned more and gained confidence from having to handle the unexpected. This is where the lessons learned stage is

DOI: 10.1201/9781003520719-8

so important. Given a similar situation, how can you mitigate the risks to prevent a similar situation from occurring?

My grown daughter and I were chatting one evening when I asked her to share the first time she thought of herself as a leader. She reminded me of an evening when she was in the ninth grade. She and her 14 best friends went out to a restaurant before attending the high school homecoming dance. Our family had two large cars and volunteered as drivers. Her father, brother, and I had dinner in a different part of the restaurant. I noticed several of her friends milling around and went to check on the rest of the girls. It turns out that each 14-year-old young woman had been given a $20 bill to purchase dinner; however, the restaurant did not offer them separate checks. One girl had ordered a steak. Two other girls had shared a salad. Even an experienced CPA would give the situation a big sigh. My daughter knew she was good at math and stepped forward to figure out the bill, manage the tip, and make change for her friends. Although she was happy to see me and glad for my offer to help her wade through the final transactions, she had done the bulk of the work before I arrived at her table. She simply needed reassurance.

I was proud of my daughter that night when she took a big breath and buckled down to work through the complicated dinner transaction. The onus lies with the parents (including me) who assumed our relatively levelheaded, honor roll daughters who had purchased movie theater tickets and meals out with a few friends would have no difficulties with the restaurant bill. None of us foresaw the complexity of a single check for 14 girls. The next year, when the group of young women attended the prehomecoming dance dinner together, they chose a restaurant that offered a prix fixe menu with four entrée choices. The bill was so much easier to navigate because they were able to take the lessons learned and devised a solution that smoothed out the unforeseen complexities from the previous year.

Change happens because the status quo is no longer working. Very few people own a crystal ball that can foresee the future. And so, it falls to formal or informal leaders who take a deep breath and forge forward into the unknown to determine a solution that may never have been done before. Or if it has, it has not been done within this type of environment or magnitude. Emotionally Intelligent leaders have experienced the personal growth that comes from navigating the uncertainty of change. They also know that if they have cultivated a strong and trusted team, they will not be alone.

SURVIVAL BY ADAPTATION

Complex change situations are often made more difficult due to a lack of leadership, procedures, and planning. Many students of organizational change look toward nature, which is full of complex biological systems, to provide metaphorical descriptions. One of my favorite examples is Stephen Johnson's description of the workings of an ant colony in his book *Emergence.* I discovered ant colonies' underground habitats are exactly the same anywhere in the world. This information is innate within the ants' DNA. Every ant habitat contains the same set of chambers. The birthing area, the food storage warehouse, the communal space, and the funerary room. All have the exact same dimensions and locations. This standardization is even more fantastic when coupled with the fact that there is no identified work supervisor. All work is performed methodically using scents to communicate. It may seem odd to bring up steadfast ant colonies in a chapter about change, but their existence is a perfect case for the concept of *survival by adaptation.*

Reading Johnson's book took me back to a vacation in Costa Rica when I observed a line of ants carrying food back to their underground storehouse. Seeing them work so hard made me feel guilty for all those ant hills I had smashed as a child. How do ants survive those random external acts which disturb their systematic way of life? The answer is simple—they persevere.

For example, if an established tunnel is suddenly impassible, the ant that encounters the blockage begins to clear an alternate path and leaves a predetermined scent marker to turn right or left for the ants that come after them. There is no established ant hierarchy to discuss the cause of the change or the various alternatives. The ant that encounters the impasse uses an innate capability to determine the necessary path and continues forward.[2]

Change has become the only constant in today's business world. Similar to the ant's survival by adaptation methodology, business leaders must learn to recognize changing situations and adapt products and services appropriately in order to thrive in increasingly complex environments. Essentially change is becoming the status quo for many organizations.

How do people adjust to constant change? Some people thrive on changes in their lives. Others prefer stability and the knowledge that everything is in its proper place. How they operate amidst change is a matter of the ways people align their choices with their personal values and preferences. Imagine what happens when an assortment of people with a variety of experiences are brought together and told that management has made decisions that will affect them and their work environment. Management-speak will describe growth opportunities, changing roles, new skill requirements as work groups are reorganized, merged, and spun off. Emotionally Intelligent leaders listen to the messages and pay attention to the reactions of the people on their team. What actions do they need to take to keep people focused on what is most important?

Often it's not the specific change that is occurring; it is the uncertainty of not knowing how people will need to shift within the new environment that is so disconcerting. People may need to reframe their perception of their place within the changing organization structure. They need time and guidance to readjust the lens they use to align their skills, knowledge, and perceived value. What behaviors will they need to adapt in order to succeed within the new environment? What new skills will be required?

CONSIDER AND DELIBERATE

Are you someone who enjoys change or do you prefer stable situations?

How do you feel when you find yourself in an opposite situation to your comfort level?

Do you prefer repetitive work assignments, or are you always the first to volunteer for a special assignment?

What is your favorite household task to perform? Why?

The final two questions may seem out of place, but if part of our goal is self-knowledge, these two are telling. Change at work will impact your personal life. How people choose to balance the two are different for each person. The key is to recognize the stress and how you will manage it. Emotionally Intelligent leaders reflect on the discomfort they are feeling as the first step toward reconciling and acclimating to the change opportunity in both their professional and personal lives. For example, for most of my professional career, I have worked on large, complex, long-term projects. Even if we could define a "done" metric, it would change before we could achieve it. My favorite household task is cleaning bathrooms. Within a 15- to 20-minute timeframe, I can see the shiny result of my efforts. There is a beginning, a middle, and a definite end to the task which is always the same. It is my way to counterbalance the constantly changing nature of my work week.

IMPROVISATION AND CHANGE

Without a doubt change is downright messy. It is difficult to plan every single detail, no matter how carefully people script the process. Change causes disruption. It may be a mild disorientation while people work through the "oops, I forgot" stage, or it could be a total chaotic disruption to what incumbent staff thought was a perfectly fine way of doing things. When things get confusing and messy, and a workable solution has yet to be realized, people will reference Friedrich Nietzsche's quote, "That which does not kill us, makes us stronger."

Tim Harford addresses the potential disorder can provide in his book *Messy: The Power of Disorder to Transform Our Lives*. He theorizes that the chaos of change pushes us to reach further into the deepest depths of our personal reserves and wrench out solutions that were never before considered. The enhanced creativity and increased resilience we acquired through this process would not have been realized had the transformation process been relatively tranquil.[3]

In hindsight, the memories of collaborative teamwork, brainstorm sessions, and applied creativity are exhilarating. When the teams who worked through the mess were able to sit back and assess their accomplishment, they all breathed a great sigh of relief. The chaos of the change process they had survived had been exhausting as they became more creative and resilient than they had ever imagined.

Many business solutions are developed through a process of theme and variation also known as improvisation. In just about every instance, people got down to the business of solution finding by trying to identify similar situations. They knew what they were asked to do had never been done before; but, they knew if they could find similarities, they could take the information forward to have a base from which they could start the solution development process and become a stronger team.

Artists use improvisation as a tool to inspire creativity and innovation. They take a simple basic theme that might be a few bars of music or a series of dance moves and create an epic work of art. They come back to the basic theme throughout the piece and then take off in a totally different direction. The constant—they always return to the theme, which can be referenced as their center or North Star to navigate their creative journey.

Often business leaders improvise when there is not time for an in-depth analysis. They have an inkling of what has worked in the past, they superimpose the current environmental situation, and they improvise a pathway from which to start the solution process. Essentially, improvisation is on-the-fly creativity. Sometimes it is successful and sometimes it is not.

Miles Davis is famous for the jazz album *A Kind of Blue*. This album which is revered among jazz aficionados was produced using a total improvisational experience. Davis had a vague idea of what he wanted, though he was dependent on the talent and experience of the musicians to help develop his basic melody sketches. Mistakes were incorporated into the recording. The finished product which was recorded over two sessions in less than nine hours was not exactly what Davis had intended; but, it became a masterpiece based on how the energies combined.

The Beatles used a different creative process than Davis used for *A Kind of Blue*. The Beatles' *Sgt. Pepper's Lonely Hearts Club Band* was recorded and produced in a series of sessions totaling 700 hours. Although each album was developed, recorded, and produced using different methodologies, both are masterful efforts. [4]

The creative process an artist chooses often is based on the amount of time available and the level of control desired by the artist. If you are a perfectionist with few time constraints, you will prefer a creation scenario that allows you the most control over the finished product.

If you have a minimal amount of time and trust your team, improvisation may be an excellent option. Like any skill, the more people practice, the stronger their improvisational skills will become. Tim Harford suggests the following exercises to hone your business-based improvisational skills.

- Accept the messiness/confusion of the situation
- Listen intently
- Let go of control, balance risk

Have you ever wondered how quickly improv comedy groups move from gathering random words from the audience to a fairly funny, somewhat complicated skit? Hours of practice helped them to develop trust and a level of comfort with each other that allows them to let go of control and adapt to the flow of the scene. Even if a comedian preferred a scene to take a different direction, they must follow the riff that their comrade began. If they are not listening intently, they may miss a cue to respond or an opportunity to make an impact and get a big laugh.[5]

CONSIDER AND DELIBERATE

Briefly describe a difficult situation that made you stronger and more resilient.

What skills did you depend on to help you survive and thrive on the challenge?

Reflect back to a situation in which you found yourself put on the spot. What were you thinking in the split seconds before you had to improvise an answer?

What steps would you take to prepare your team to improvise a solution to a complicated situation?

Even the most detailed business plan will not guarantee that change will not occur. The first action to take when faced with a complicated situation is to take at least two very deep breaths. The purpose of these two deep breaths is to get oxygen to the brain so you can think more clearly. The two breaths also are contagious. The people near you will begin to take a breath. Breathing allows everyone to focus their attention and begin to improvise a solution.

LEADING THROUGH THE PARADOXES OF CHANGE

Whether working within an improvisational mode or developing well-thought plans, leaders within changing organizations need to guide and align a shifting multi-layered mosaic. There will be times when leaders find themselves managing a variety of inconsistencies as they try to balance the demands to achieve both short and long-term goals. Wendy K. Smith and her research team reference these multidimensional practices as Paradoxical Leadership. Using improvisational strategies, leaders are able to create an organizational mindset that enables team players to create an abundance of possibilities from the same set of resources that traditional leaders label as scarce.

Instead of making trade-offs that provide multiple groups thinner and thinner slices of the resource pie, paradoxical leaders look to grow the pie exponentially through collaborative strategies and resource reframing for flexible outcomes. And thus, the paradox—how do some people given the same resources and similar scenarios create so much more value? The answer is that successful leaders recognize and address each element/layer of the dynamic organization mosaic which incorporates:

- Multiple Values
- Variety of Contributions
- Unique Differentiators

Paradoxical leaders embrace the messiness of change and open themselves to opportunity and possibility. They leverage experimentation, critical feedback, and continuous tuning as they guide their teams toward a solution. Their secret weapon is a variation on the improvisational game, "Yes, and." When improv groups play this game, one person starts with a statement such as, "Let's pack a picnic and go to the beach." It doesn't matter if the second person would much prefer the mountains, they must agree and add another element to the story. The second person might say, "Yes, and we'll stop on the way to buy rocket launchers to use after dark." The story builds and expands.

Wendy Smith and her team categorize traditional leadership approaches as using "Either/Or" strategies and the paradoxical leadership approach as using "Both/And." Table 8.1 compares the various behaviors of these two types of leaders summarized by people who focus on allocation trade-offs and people who explore opportunities to enhance the value of current resources.[6]

TABLE 8.1

Paradoxical Leadership Matrix

"Either/Or" Leaders	"Both/And" Leaders
Acts Consistently	Acts Consistently Inconsistent
Makes Strategic Choices	Simultaneously Engages in Conflicting Strategies
Sets a Clear Agenda	Searches for Opportunities to Grow Resources
Makes Allocation Trade-Offs	Sets Flexible Time Frames
Adopts Consistent Identity Across Organization	Embraces Multiple Strategies and Identities
Promotes Best Practices	Tolerates Uncertainty
Keeps It Simple	Learns From Failure

CONSIDER AND DELIBERATE

Describe a situation when you used an "either/or" strategy.

Describe a situation when you used a "both/and" strategy.

How satisfied were you with each outcome?

Reflecting back, did you notice a difference in the support other people provided?

There will be times when it is the best strategy for a leader to deploy traditional leadership skills to drive strong team performance. However, when people are juggling multiple priorities, organizational complexities, and the multi-layered effects that occur with change, Emotionally Intelligent leaders employ the abundance of paradoxical leadership strategies to best support their teams through confusion and uncertainty.

CHANGE, TRANSITIONS, AND UNCERTAINTY

When several organizational groups or teams merge, the complexity of the ensuing uncertainty exacerbates. What ties this group of individuals together? How are multiple contributions linked together? Will various groups overlap? People may suddenly split their time between two managers. How will work priorities be negotiated across workgroups?

These disagreements are not necessarily negative and will soon become the "new normal." And so, in addition to trying to realign their professional pursuits, people start to wonder how established workplace social norms will change. What will happen to the norms and traditions that surround daily coffee klatches, lunch breaks, and informal watercooler conversations? How will they shift? The effect on their informal social group may have a greater impact on them than the official organizational change announcement.

Working through change, team members, as well as leaders need to gain confidence as they address the accompanying uncertainties. Stephen Heidari-Robinson and Suzanne Heywood cited a McKinnsey study that surveyed 1,800 executives regarding the most common reorganizational pitfalls in their article "Getting Reorgs Right." Employees resisting change were cited as the number one reason why reorganizations failed. Why do people find change to be so difficult? The author's research indicates that two-thirds of company reorganizations provide some business improvement. In light of a positive potential, why are employees resistant to change that can deliver positive results? The short answer most often is how the mission, goals, and process that drive the reorganization are communicated. Other reasons can be attributed to previous change experiences in which they carry forward memories from prior failed experiences cited by the McKinnsey results which include:

- Insufficient people, time, and money dedicated to the reorganization effort
- Individual productivity declines because of distractions from day-to-day operations
- Organizational chart changes do not filter down to the functional level
- Unforeseen consequences (such as expanded IT requirements) derail the implementation plans

FIGURE 8.1
Systematic reorganization approach.

Heidari-Robinson and Heywood recommend that organizations take a systematic approach when planning a reorganization process that has a significantly greater chance for success. Figure 8.1 illustrates the flow of the systematic process to best realize successful results. The first item to remember is that a reorganization process is about making a change to the business. It is not just about moving people around. Executives need to construct a profit/loss statement for the endeavor. What are the costs? What are the benefits? What are opportunities? And, what are the risks?

The second step is to review the strengths and weaknesses of your resources. Where are the gaps? What level of investment is required? Will you need to hire additional people? What type of internal training will be needed?

The third step is to determine how the changes will be implemented. Will the changes be deployed from the top down or functionally from the bottom up? Will you have a beta group as an initial test group from which to learn and adapt the plan before a full out implementation?

The fourth step is to clarify the implementation stages to make sure that resources are available when needed. The fifth and final step is to monitor the change process carefully so that mistakes can be corrected, any adjustments verified, and the reorganization plan updated to clarify the learned changes.[7]

Very often reorganizations and other types of changes happen because someone suggests a good idea and it expands into a reality before the details can be thought through, much less a plan developed. A Nigerian folktale explaining why the sun and moon live in the sky is an example of how the consequences from an idea that is not well thought out can have a long-term impact.

Many years ago, Sun and Water were great friends. They both lived on the earth together and Sun would visit the Water at his home; however, Water did not visit Sun. One day, Sun asked Water why he never visited the Sun's house. Water responded, he needed to travel with all of his people and Sun's house was not big enough to hold them all. Sun went back to the house he shared with his wife, Moon, and began to build a huge compound for Water and his people to visit. When he finished building the compound, he invited Water to come for a visit.

The next day Water arrived and began to flow into the compound Sun had built. Soon, Water and all of the fish and sea animals began to overflow the compound. Water asked Sun if it was still safe for him and his wife. Sun, being very polite, answered, "of course, you and your friends are most welcome." Water and his friends continued flowing. Soon the water level had reached the top of Sun's head. He stood on a chair to remain safe. Water called out again to determine if Sun and Moon were safe. They were very polite people and wanted to welcome their friend and responded, "of course, you are most welcome." The water kept flowing until Sun and Moon were perched on the top of the roof. They felt it would be impolite to stop their friend and his friends from entering their home and would not call a stop to the flowing water. Finally, they were forced into the sky, where they remained ever since.[8]

Sun had the very best of intentions, but he did not realize the immenseness of the sea. Water made checks regarding the wellbeing of Sun and Moon, but they were too polite to withdraw their original invitation. This is exactly what can happen during reorganization. The initial suggestion sounds like a great idea. Unforeseen circumstances can happen and if no one identifies the impact on the original plan negative outcomes will occur.

Brainstorm planning sessions are excellent for helping people think outside of the proverbial box; however, no idea should be taken forward until it is properly vetted. My "wish I had stopped it" story happened during a meeting that was supposed to determine the next new technology for a training curriculum. I threw out an esoteric concept expecting everyone to shut it down. They surprised me by unanimously voting it forward. It was a disaster. Not a single person registered for the pilot course. Fortunately, the time and money lost from the failed effort was minimal.

CONSIDER AND DELIBERATE

Reflect back to a time when an off-the-cuff suggestion you made to your friends or within a professional brainstorming session was determined to be the "perfect idea." What were your initial feelings?

Did you try to discourage the group from carrying the idea forward?

What was the final outcome?

What sort of memories do you have regarding that event today?

Although an idea may initially seem to be "really" good, Emotionally Intelligent leaders guide their teams to more fully explore the possible consequences and identify actions that could minimize negative outcomes.

UNCERTAINTY AND ADAPTATION

Reorganization is just one of the types of changes businesses encounter throughout their lifecycle. Similar to natural organisms, businesses must adapt in order to survive changing environments. In the article "The Biology of Corporate Survival," Martin Reeves, a senior partner at the Boston Consulting Group, Simon Levin, a Professor of Biology at Princeton University, and Daichi Ueda, an associate at the Boston Consulting Group, merged their disciplines to explore how 21st-century organizations can prepare to address unpredictable environmental risks and ward off organizational threats that can cause their demise. Their research acknowledges three complex trends that increase an organization's uncertainty and risk:

1. Unpredictable business environments
2. Shorter, fast-paced technology change and integration cycles
3. Global partner interdependencies for which local businesses have exposure with minimal control

The authors' concern is based on the complexity of today's business environment and the inability of organizations to recognize and adapt to shifting circumstances. Their recommendation to organizations trying to prepare a resilient foundation is to expect surprise, but reduce uncertainty.

Paying attention to the full environment allows leaders to recognize details that could signal change. They suggest a strategy of employing a heterogeneous staff from diverse backgrounds whose depth of experience enables the team to visualize possible outcomes and prepare actions to mitigate negative consequences. Regular feedback loops and modular reporting structures will enable organizations to adapt and respond as needed to unexpected changes.

One example they discuss is The Montreal Protocol which is an international treaty designed to protect the ozone layer. Scientists from around the world shared hard data that analyzed the impact of fluorocarbons and the depleting ozone layer on human health. They lobbied international governments and businesses to take action and the result is large-scale international co-operation for which the results demonstrate a measurable restorative impact on the atmosphere. Since the initial accord was passed in 1987, The Montreal Protocol has undergone eight revisions to address new information realized through the monitoring process and continues to be considered one of the most successful international agreements.

The lessons the business sector can take from this is to actively monitor market environments to become aware of small signals that could negatively impact your organization. Well-established market leaders make a mistake when they rest on the laurels that took them to their market leader position. Ignoring your competitors' actions, and especially the innovations from small new market entrants is a signal that you have stopped adapting and may not survive as a company, much less your market leader status.[9]

Adaptation requires leaders to recognize that they, their staff, and even the functional structure of their organization can be improved. In fact, uncertainty can be seen as an opportunity to give your organization a diagnostic once over and reframe some long-held ideas as the first steps toward innovation and growth.

REFRAMING UNCERTAINTY

The first step toward addressing uncertain situations is to try to find a common understanding. This may take the form of viewing the situation from a different perspective which many call reframing. The benefit of viewing the situation from a different angle is that you might discover additional information that you have not yet considered. This information may help you identify some potential solutions or options for action that can be explored, evaluated, and drive well-informed decisions.

Reframing is a corollary to the adage "if your only tool is a hammer, every problem requires a nail." This is the strength of collaborative learning. Discussing the circumstances and resolution possibilities among several people provides the opportunity to explore a situation from a variety of perspectives. Someone might bring up a possible consequence no one had considered. A solution that is cheaper, faster, and provides improved quality might just be the outcome from these creative conversations.

And sometimes the solution is so simple that it is overlooked. The reframing process might help to cut away complicated operations that evolved over months or years. A fresh set of eyes often is able to see the obvious that no one was able to recognize. The story about the young boy who told the emperor he was wearing no clothes illustrates this point. A self-proclaimed haute-couture tailor traveled through the kingdom and asked to see the emperor so he could make him an outfit of the most beautiful fabrics. The emperor was a bit vain and enjoyed wearing beautiful clothes and invited the tailor to stay at the palace while this beautiful outfit was made. The tailor secreted himself away and would let no one see the outfit until it was complete. On the day of the grand unveiling, the tailor carried what looked like an empty hanger into the emperor's chambers. The tailor immediately asked the emperor what he thought of this beautiful outfit made of gold and silver fabrics. Not wanting to appear stupid, he went along with the tailor. The tailor personally dressed him using elaborate pantomime. The emperor's closest advisors were called in to see this most elaborate outfit. The advisors immediately began to praise the beautiful fabrics the tailor was describing to them because they did not want to appear stupid and unworldly.

Someone suggested the emperor should walk about his kingdom so all of the citizens of his realm could admire his new finery. As the emperor walked through the main square, a young boy called out, "The emperor is not wearing any clothes!" Guards immediately snagged the young man. The emperor called out for him to be let go because he was telling the truth—he wasn't wearing anything but his undergarments. He had been a vain and foolish old man who had been duped into believing something that was not true. He called for the fraudulent tailor who was nowhere to be found. He chastised his advisors for telling him what they thought he wanted to hear and praised the young boy for his courage and honesty.

The young boy was not a global fashion expert. He simply stated what he saw. The complicated description spun by the tailor and the court sophisticates of what they thought they were supposed to see was nothing but a fraud. This simple tale is a parable for what can happen when complex, multi-faceted organizations are confronted with what appears to be complicated decisions. It is important to promote simple conversations that assure understanding of the root cause of the problem and not limit efforts to resolving the symptoms.

ACTIVE LISTENING

Active listening is a crucial behavioral component for successful leaders. It involves both questioning and listening. How many times have you attended a meeting or a social function, where you can honestly say you are providing the other person your absolute full attention? An active listener provides the other person(s) their full attention and demonstrates this by asking probing questions and listening to the entire answer before commenting. The goal of the conversational interchange is to reach a full understanding of the event, process, or challenge at hand.

How often do people "assume away" complexity? They take information at face value without pausing to see if there might be some sort of challenge lurking in the shadows. There is a story that describes a situation where people ignored subtle symptoms that did not seem serious, at first.

Steve, the factory supervisor, sees a puddle on the floor and calls for Joe to mop it up. Later that afternoon, he sees the puddle again and calls out to Joe, "I told you to mop up that mess, why didn't you do it?" Joe mumbles he did already, and shuffles off to get the mop. Not once does Steve question the source of the puddle. The next morning, the workers arrive to find the entire floor flooded. In researching the cause of the flood, it was discovered that the prior weekend a windstorm had knocked over a large structure that cracked the roof when it fell. The puddle was formed by water leaking through the roof. A major rainstorm had come through during the night. The tiles could no longer support the weight of the water as it gushed into the ceiling enclosure during the storm.

If Steve had stopped to research the source of the recurring puddle instead of demanding a quick fix to the symptom, the leaking roof may have been diagnosed and an expensive incident avoided. When dealing with multiple layers that support complex systems, people assume obvious symptoms as the actual cause for the challenge at hand and ignore the possibility the problem could be a consequence of a deeper predicament.

Emotionally Intelligent leaders demonstrate their strength when they are able to express confidence in the different working groups' success and align the separate efforts to achieve the organizational vision.

CONSIDER AND DELIBERATE

Has a manager or another influential person in your life dominated the conversation, assuming their situation was exactly the same as the one you were experiencing?

What was your reaction? How did the scene play out? Given another opportunity, what do you wish had happened?

Think about the managers, leaders, or colleagues who impressed you. How did they help you work toward complex solutions?

Albert Einstein is quoted as saying, "If I were given one hour to save the planet, I would spend 59 minutes defining the problem and one minute resolving it." Many times the solution reveals itself when people take the time to ask questions as part of the process to identify the root cause of a problem. Emotionally Intelligent leaders gather people who have a variety of viewpoints and expertise to resolve complex situations. Examining a problem from several angles offers a better chance that the actual root cause will be discovered and resolved.

DOUBLE LOOP LEARNING

Chris Argyris and Donald Schon, researchers in action-oriented organizational learning, developed a Double Loop Learning Model to help people address uncertainty and resolve complex problems. Double loop learning as illustrated in Figure 8.2 is a series of iterative, interconnecting decision stage loops. The basic premise of Double Loop Learning is that each time a problem situation is viewed from a different perspective or a different analytical method is tried, we learn a little bit more about the problem and the eventual solution. The five-phase learning process—Intention, Evaluation, Feedback, Decision, and Action—is designed as individual iterative functions.

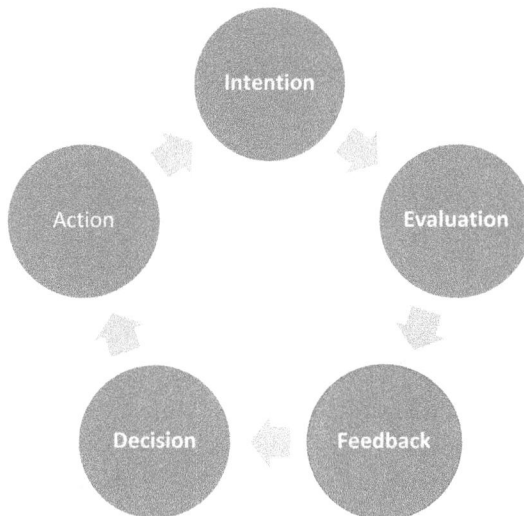

FIGURE 8.2
Double loop learning model.

For example, when contemplating how to make a significant change within your organization, it is important to carefully define the intention. What is the purpose or ultimate goal of the new program? Moving forward into the evaluation stage, review the current environment and identify the various methods to create the new program. What are the financial and procedural options/challenges?

During the feedback stage, identify people who will be affected by the change and people who may have already worked through a similar process. Add their feedback to the information you gathered during the evaluation period. Have you not considered an important planning element? Are your priorities aligned properly? Are you asking the right questions and thinking about the right things?[10]

Once you've reviewed the feedback and begun to hone your plan, select a pilot or beta project as an initial test for the change action. If the trial action is successful, then you can begin to move toward the final decision and deployment phase.

This model is relatively flexible and can be applied in almost every situation. For example, you may discover during the evaluation phase that the budget required to fully implement your intended change is much too expensive. You don't necessarily need to give up your mission. Your initial effort was not wrong, You have new budget limitations and will need to scale back the original plan.

As you move from one phase to another, it is important to review the plans to make sure that the activity/project continues to align with the organization's mission and that schedules and staffing resources are coordinated.

DOUBLE LOOP LEARNING AND PERSONAL GROWTH

Emotionally Intelligent leaders utilize double loop learning strategies to assure that they take the time to reflect and adapt to changing circumstances. What new skills and connections are needed to succeed? The strength of double loop learning is the anchor it provides for growth during uncertainty and change.

Most first days involve a great many challenges and unknowns that require navigation. Apprehension and excitement are normal feelings for first days. By the end of the first day, some people have a well-mapped-out course, but, more often than not, people leave feeling a bit overwhelmed by the procedures and acronyms that come so naturally to colleagues at the new organization.

Experienced leaders advise new leaders coming into an organization to embrace the uncertainty initially. They recommend that people watch and observe the culture, the processes, and how people work, before making any changes. Once you understand the organization and the people within it, you will make wiser suggestions which should be received more readily than if you immediately began making slash-and-burn changes.

Last days also can be difficult for a very different reason. No matter how exciting your next position may be, there is much comfort in being familiar with an organization's rhythms. The procedures and acronyms that were so foreign on your first day are second nature to you. Somewhere between your first and your last day, you experienced an individual learning curve.

CONSIDER AND DELIBERATE

Remember back to a "first day." It could be your first day at a new job or assignment. What were you feeling? What was your perception of the environment?

At the end of your first 30 days in this position, how had you changed? Did your perception of the environment change? Did you make changes to your performance or behavior during the previous weeks? Why?

By your one-year anniversary, how have you changed? Has your perception of the environment changed? Did you make changes to your performance or behavior during the previous months? Why?

What about your last day at that job or project? (If you selected a current project, describe your current thoughts.) What were you feeling? What was the perception of the environment?

What occurred between your first day and your last day that shifted your feelings?

During change situations, both individuals and organizations must work through learning curves which aren't always synchronized. Individual learning can be just as complex as organizational learning.

Not all people within an organization learn in the same way and at the same pace. Emotionally Intelligent leaders pay attention to the pace of the various learning rhythms. If the individual and organizational learning curves get too far out of sync, leaders need to step in to assure everyone, even in the midst of uncertainty, maintains the same trajectory alignment as they work toward their goals.

RISK, UNCERTAINTY, AND PLANNING OPPORTUNITIES

There is always an element of risk in even the most simplistic of management decisions. What is the possibility that the project/event will be successful? Or, conversely, what is the possibility that it will fail? The role of a leader is to address risk directly head-on. Emotionally Intelligent leaders spend the bulk of their time managing opportunities and expectations. They must forecast impending obstacles, identify the likelihood and significance of the impact, and mitigate any negative possibilities to ensure a positive outcome.

When you face a change situation, uncertainty adds an additional risk element to the decision-making process. Traditional risk management addresses the impact a proposed change will have on organizational resources and procedures. Risk/benefit analysis is fairly similar whether you are reviewing a simple solution for a predictable change outcome or a project that involves many moving parts and carries a significant amount of uncertainty.

The challenge to developing and deploying a solution for a complex conundrum is the necessity for people to address the range of potential solutions from a multidimensional lens. When the problem resolution process is based on multiple viewpoints, the final solution will be more robust with a greater potential for achievement since it addresses a total organizational perspective. Involving representatives from the entire organization in different aspects of the change process will also help to assure a successful change transition. Figure 8.3 illustrates the risk analysis procedures

FIGURE 8.3
Unpredictable and predictable risk matrix.

applied to predictable change situations and the additional layers of analysis driven by multiple lenses that overlay the basic process as people strive to create innovative solutions in an effort to minimize uncertainty.[11]

Every individual or organizational situation is different, in some way. Each time you are confronted by an "opportunity," whether positive or negative, ask the following questions:

- Is this a risk that needs to be addressed?
- What is the driving basis of this "opportunity"?
- How will this affect the current organizational culture?
- Who needs to be part of the discussion and planning?
- What message needs to be communicated? When? And to whom?

Your answer to these questions will determine whether the situation is routine with a predictable outcome, or if you will need to use multiple lenses to develop an innovative solution.

The first step toward risk assessment is to determine the significance of the "opportunity" and how it will affect the goal being pursued. Taking the time to perform this evaluation enables leaders to keep people focused on what is important and set aside what is not important. When a suggestion is presented as a positive benefit, the evaluation criteria should incorporate how the activity aligns with the organization mission (benefits) and the people and financial resource requirements to pursue the activity (costs). It is important to consider what is motivating the person who is bringing this wonderful opportunity to the table. How will each party benefit?

When the risk introduces a problem, it is important to gather as much information as quickly as possible to understand the significance of the negative impact. How badly will the planned activity be impeded? Is it a minor issue that is a distraction, or is the situation one which could change the direction of the project?

Once you have the facts and can identify the root cause and not just the symptoms, you and your team will be able to evaluate the situation rationally and then will be able to identify several possible strategies to resolve the situation.

Vijay Govindarajan, a professor at Dartmouth's Tuck School of Business, refers to these risk evaluation activities as Planned Opportunism. His theory encourages people to mitigate the discomfort and worry that stem from uncertainty by preparing for those challenges that can be predicted. Because people are able to exert some level of control in the face of uncertainty, they will not be as disturbed by an unplanned situation that does not have an immediate resolution. They are able to maintain a productive level of calm because they are prepared to take action. Teams are able to pursue possible resolutions with the knowledge that they are being as proactive as possible. The power of this technique to take control of uncertainty is the confidence people gain as they begin to develop their own change culture.[12]

COLLABORATIVE RESOLUTION

The diversity of the team participating in problem resolution discussions and planning has a direct correlation with the success of the outcome of the decision solution. Everyone brings their personal experience and a certain amount of bias to every dialogue. It is important to include representatives from all of the organizations who could be affected by the problem or the solution.

Communications regarding the problem/solution should not wait until the implementation process is underway. The timing of communications is as important as the message you are sending out. You don't want the rumor mill to be anyone's information source. An established set of procedures that can automatically be deployed when an unexpected situation occurs will help you maintain control of the message context and format that people both inside and outside of your organization receive.

Have you ever shared good news with someone you swore to secrecy and heard it coming back at you on the grapevine? Had the meaning of the message changed? How much damage control was required? Could any of the energies required to "make things right" been avoided if you had stopped for a moment to consider the risks?

CONSIDER AND DELIBERATE

Briefly outline the circumstances surrounding an unexpected "opportunity" you encountered over the past 3 months.

What criteria did you use to evaluate the situation?

How would this "opportunity" affect the originally planned outcome?

Who did you consult to help you determine the best solution? What is their role? Did you follow their advice? Why, or why not?

When and how did you share the "opportunity" and the various resolution stages with interested parties?

Risk assessment, mitigation, and communication can be complicated even for relatively straightforward situations. The complexity of these procedures exponentially expands when multiple departments and organizations need to be brought into risk prevention and resolution discussions. Who, when, and how become significant details that require advanced attention.

In summary, change does not occur in a vacuum. The consequences from one action can create unanticipated consequences in other areas. Emotionally Intelligent leaders must constantly be alert to positive or negative "opportunities," address them as they arise, and find the best people available to anticipate an appropriate resolution.

This chapter explored strategies to manage uncertainty and change. Double loop learning is a strategy that can be used for both organizational and individual growth. The next chapter focuses on the human element that is the essence of an Emotionally Intelligent leader.

NOTES

1 Grant, Adam. (2016). *Origins.* (pp. 12–13). New York, NY: Penguin Books.

2 Johnson, Stephen. (2002). *Emergence: The Connected Lives of Ants, Brains, Cities, and Software.* (pp. 29–33) Scribner: New York, NY.

3 Harford, Tim. (2016). *Messy: The Power of Disorder to Transform Our Lives.* (p. 5). Riverhead Books. New York, NY.

4 Harford, Tim. (2016). *Messy: The Power of Disorder to Transform Our Lives.* (pp. 95–98). Riverhead Books. New York, NY.

5 Harford, Tim. (2016). *Messy: The Power of Disorder to Transform Our Lives.* (pp. 109–111). Riverhead Books. New York, NY.

6 Smith, Wendy K., Lewis, Marianne W., and Tushman, Michael L. (May 2016). "Both/And" Leadership. *Harvard Business Review.* (pp. 63–70).

7 Heidari-Robinson and Heywood, Suzanne (November 2016). "A Practical Guide to a Misunderstood—And Often Mismanaged—Process." *Harvard Business Review.* pp. 85–89.

8 Elphinstone Dayrell, (1910). *Folk Stories From Southern Nigeria.* Retrieved January 27, 2017, from http://www.sacred-texts.com/afr/fssn/fsn18.htm

9 Reeves, Martin, Levin, Simon, and Ueda, Daicihi. (January/February 2016). "The Biology of Corporate Survival." *Harvard Business Review.* p. 55.

10 Morgan, Gareth. (2006). *Images of Organization.* (p. 84–89). Thousand Oaks, CA: Sage Publications.

11 © 2017 by Susan Schwartz of the River Birch Group. Reprinted with permission.

12 Govindarajan, Vijay. (November 2016). "Planned Opportunism." *Harvard Business Review.* p. 61.

CHAPTER SUMMARY

Growth and Uncertainty

- Organizations must learn to recognize changing situations and adapt products and services appropriately to survive within increasingly complex environments.

- People's discomfort with change is often more about the uncertainty of not knowing how the "story" will end than the actual change that is being deployed.
- Collaborative consultation and improvisation can bring creativity to the solution and avoid missteps.
- Effective change leaders incorporate multiple values, consult diverse points of view, and identify unique differentiators.
- The primary reason why reorganization efforts fail is due to employees' resistance to change. Communications aligning the organization mission, goals, and processes with the change effort can help to gain employee support.
- Reorganizations change the business and should not be initiated without developing a well-thought-out plan identifying all costs and benefits.
- Uncertainty is an opportunity to review and reframe long-held views.
- Examining a problem from several angles offers a better chance to discover and resolve the actual root cause.

9

Leaders Are Human Too

> Leaders enable good power ethics by…
> Alpha leaders can…
> Reflective learning action cycles drive…

Leaders are the ones who people count on to make things happen. Being the person to whom everyone looks toward for that new idea or what to do when the going gets tough is difficult work—and can be daunting. The load will become heavy and seem unmanageable, if you try to carry everything solely on your shoulders. It is important for you, an Emotionally Intelligent leader, to remember that humans will make mistakes navigating unfamiliar territory and that you need to give yourself grace. Practice forgiving yourself, your role models, and the people who work with you for mistakes and perceived weaknesses—after all, we are all human too.

TRUE LEADERSHIP

Carlo Rovelli, a quantum gravity physicist, aptly describes this quest for achievement in the preface of his book *Reality Is Not What It Seems: The Journey to Quantum Gravity*. He writes, "This is not a book about certainties; it is a book about the adventure of moving towards the unknown."[1] This is what true leadership is about; it isn't about following well-defined rules.

It's about helping people navigate the unknown to achieve something that others might consider improbable, if not impossible.

DOI: 10.1201/9781003520719-9

At the end of the day leadership is defined by the people who travel the journey together. It is about maintaining alignment among the various organizational parts in order to achieve the shared mission and vision as a whole. It is not about taking the path less traveled as the poet Robert Frost suggests. It is about forging new paths by leveraging the strengths of your team to build the necessary roads and bridges.

During an interview, Rovelli described physics as a means of understanding the world, "I think we shouldn't reduce it to things. We should reduce it to a happening, and the happenings are always between different systems, always relations. Or always, like a kiss, which is something that happens between two persons."[2] Similar to physics, leadership is not about a person or a single group. Leaders need to be aware of the interconnections between organizational systems and the relationships that connect people to make success happen.

PARADOXICAL BEHAVIORS

Dacher Keltner, a professor of psychology at the University of California at Berkeley, researched executive behavior patterns over a 20-year period to discover how people make success happen. He uncovered a troubling pattern that appeared in almost every study which he named the *power paradox*. This paradox describes a phenomenon that appears in a large number of executives who rise through formal leadership ranks, practicing leadership "superpowers" and demonstrating traits such as empathy, collaboration, transparency, humility, and sharing. Once these leaders attained a position of power, they began to enjoy the accompanying privilege, and the qualities that helped them to rise through the ranks began to wane.

People who only a few months earlier had exhibited positive leadership traits were now described as boorish. People who once placed the needs of others before their own were seen endorsing selfish and unethical actions. Even more interesting is the impact that rude and selfish behaviors have on organizational productivity. Half of the people who responded to a poll, with 800 manager participants across 17 industries, admitted to purposefully decreasing their work effort as a response to being treated rudely by a higher ranking organizational official.

Once Keltner realized the pervasiveness of the power paradox, he began to search for a means that could help executives avoid succumbing to these privileged behaviors. He discovered that people who recognized trigger warnings (e.g. frustration) were able to address their feelings in a logical manner. These executives were less likely to behave rudely and more likely to exhibit constructive behaviors.

Keltner developed a series of practices he describes as "the ethics of good power" to help executives promote positive behaviors. The three practices of empathy, gratitude, and generosity are lane markers that can help leaders expand their ability to engage in simple relationship-building behaviors. Table 9.1 illustrates several suggestions to help practice the ethics of good power.[3]

People notice everything about a leader's verbal, written, and non-verbal communications. In preparing this book, I asked many people to describe leaders who made an impression on them. A friend who works for a global technology company described her regional vice president. He visits the local office once every 4–8 weeks and makes a practice of walking around and saying good morning to each person in the office with appropriate small talk or memory from a previous visit. Although he might spend the rest of the day in a series of meetings, he always takes 15–20 minutes to meet and greet the local employees before he begins his day. Previous regional vice-presidents didn't extend this simple gesture to the staff. Their habit was to come into the office and get right to work. In our discussion, she believed the previous regional vice-presidents were fine managers who were focused on doing their jobs well; however, when she was asked to describe a leader, she didn't think about the manager who drove the

TABLE 9.1

Good Power Ethics

Good Power Ethic	Suggested Practices
EMPATHY	• Listen with your body turned toward and focused on speaker. • Ask questions and paraphrase the answer you hear to confirm your understanding. • Before meetings, take a moment to review what is happening in the life of the person with whom you will meet.
GRATITUDE	• Publicly thank people for their efforts and contributions. • Send colleagues emails or traditional thank you notes to appreciate a job well done. • Celebrate small successes as well as the really big wins.
GENEROSITY	• Share the limelight and recognize everyone who contributed. • Delegate important and high-profile responsibilities to staff. • Seek opportunities to spend one-on-one time with people on your team.

highest numbers, she thought of the person who noticed and appreciated the people who worked within his organization.

CONSIDER AND DELIBERATE

Reflect on a time when you were involved in a power paradox situation. Were you the person who received the privileged reward, or did you observe someone else assume a privilege as described by the power paradox?

Briefly describe the situation and include any thoughts or feelings you remember from the event. Would you behave differently today?

Describe the last time you practiced *empathy* during a professional or volunteer group activity. How did you feel at the time?

Describe the last time you practiced *gratitude* during a professional or volunteer group activity. How did you feel at the time?

Describe the last time you practiced *generosity* during a professional or volunteer group activity. How did you feel at the time?

Good power practices are Emotionally Intelligent motivational habits to help build relationships within your organization. The 15–20 minutes the regional vice-president spent informally visiting with staff at the field office was an effective team-building investment. In addition to letting the local staff know they are valued, the corporate officer was able to gain a snapshot of the local office culture. If there is an unsettling trend that requires higher level attention, the regional vice-president has established a baseline of the office culture and trust of the local staff should he need to make specific queries.

ALPHA PERSONALITY TRAPS

Are you an Alpha leader or a Beta leader? Traditionally, executive positions were held by people who exhibited excessively ambitious and competitive Alpha or A-type personalities. Aspiring executives were encouraged to develop aggressive, tightly controlled management approaches which are often associated with Alpha-type leaders. Beta or B-Type leaders are not as aggressive as Alpha-type personalities and are noted for their collaborative work styles.

Kate Ludeman and Eddie Erlandson, authors of the *Alpha Male Syndrome* (2006), determined through their research that 70% of all senior executives could be classified as successful, Alpha-types. The executive profile developed by the research reflected people who enjoyed the stress and responsibilities of being in charge of making the "tough" decisions. For example, Alpha-type executives are described as being able to act decisively and have strong intuition which allows them to make quick decisions.

As Ludeman and Erlandson explored the various characteristics of Alpha-type executive behaviors, they learned the traits that have long been considered strengths for organizational leaders also could prove hazardous for organization growth within fast, changing environments. The traits that enable Alpha-types to be self-confident and opinionated also can cause them to be close-minded, domineering, and intimidating when they find themselves in a collaborative situation in which they are not the sole decision-maker. Their action-oriented traits that enable them to drive results also can cause them to appear impatient and resistant to process changes that are not immediately evident. Seven common Alpha-type attributes are listed in Table 9.2 alongside the associated potential values and risks these behaviors bring to an organization.

Collaborative practices, which are innate to Beta-type leaders, are very difficult for Alpha-type leaders to perform. Ludeman's team has successfully coached many Alpha executives to become more effective leaders by helping them to become aware of their behaviors which could put the effectiveness and productivity of their organizations at risk. The basic premise is that in order for executive leaders to grow and change, they must take the time to become aware of their personal motivators, accept

TABLE 9.2

Alpha Value/Risk Matrix

Alpha Attribute	Value	Risk
Self-Confident/ Opinionated	Acts decisively	Closed minded and intimidating
Highly Intelligent	Sees beyond the obvious	Dismisses and demeans colleagues who disagree
Action-Oriented	Produces results	Impatient; Resists process changes for improved results
High Performance Expectation	Sets and achieves high goals	Constantly dissatisfied; Fails to appreciate/motivate others
Direct Communication Style	Moves people to action	Generates fear and CYA culture of compliance
Highly Disciplined	Extraordinarily productive	Has unreasonable expectations; Misses signs of burnout
Unemotional	Laser focused and objective	Is difficult to connect with; Does not inspire teams

they will not have all of the answers, and explore new perspectives and contrary opinions.

Their approach targets five goals for their clients to practice as they hone their Alpha attributes and learn how to successfully lead a collaborative 21st-century workforce. The first goal is for the executive to admit vulnerability and begin to ask people for assistance. The second goal is to accept accountability for their impact on other people's performance. Type-A executives often don't recognize that their decisions can have an adverse impact on other people and departments within the organization. The third goal is to help the Type-A executive acknowledge and learn how to constructively manage their emotions.

Learning how to balance positive and negative feedback is the fourth goal of the coaching process. Ludeman's team discovered that 80% of the feedback Alpha personality types deliver to their team focuses on negative measures. The purpose of the fourth goal is to help Type-A executives learn how to blend appreciative comments into their feedback flow so they can more effectively motivate and move their teams forward using a combination of critical and positive comments. The fifth and final goal of Ludeman's coaching process is to help executives recognize patterns associated with destructive behaviors. By helping an executive understand the root cause of their poor behaviors, s/he is able to let go of their defensive mode and become a leader who can help teams to focus on a constructive resolution.[4]

CONSIDER AND DELIBERATE

Do you work with an Alpha-type person in a professional or volunteer capacity? Briefly describe a challenge that you find difficult to manage when working together with them on a task.

> How might you encourage them to recognize and address one of Ludeman's five goals (vulnerability, accountability, managing emotions, balanced feedback, and pattern recognition) to help Alpha-type people become stronger collaborative leaders?

Both Alpha and Beta personality type executives can become strong leaders. The type of person who is best suited to lead a group will depend on the specific situation. While Alpha leaders need to practice delegating and working collaboratively, Beta personality types often can get caught up in the discussions and need to be coached to draw boundaries. Dr. Dana Ardi, author of *The Fall of the Alphas: The New Beta Way to Connect, Collaborate, Influence, and Lead,* describes several Beta-type leaders and the collaborative relationships they maintain with their "second-in-command." One of the most famous of this type of partnership is between Warren Buffett, Berkshire Hathaway CEO, and Charlie Munger, Berkshire Hathaway Vice Chairman. Berkshire Hathaway is an American multinational conglomerate holding company headquartered in Omaha Nebraska. Buffett and Munger have worked together since 1982 and describe their roles within the company as co-strategists, kindred spirits, and intellectual sparring partners who have developed a very efficient learning machine between them.[5]

The U.S. military places a high priority on leadership development. Battlefield generals have to make split-second decisions that have repercussions. Business leaders often look to the military for Alpha-focused role models. The less successful business leaders identify the efficiency and don't recognize the care and humility that the military tradition holds as a priority. The next section describes several examples of the human behind U.S. military generals and their alpha-based decisions.

MILITARY GENERALS AND MINDFULNESS

Prior to reading *The Generals: American Military Command from World War II to Today* by Thomas Ricks, I believed the stereotype that military officers were all extreme Alpha-type leaders. I purchased the book so that I could better relate to the growing number of people transitioning out of the military who were attending my project management classes. Even though I can say "some of my best friends" served in the armed forces, I only had a superficial understanding of military organizations. I hoped that Ricks' book would provide me with a better understanding of military strategy, the combat experience, and the impact of technology. Yes, I learned a great deal about those topics; however, my greatest takeaway was an entirely new paradigm of what it takes to be a successful leader, one that can be applied in any type of organization: military, corporate, not-for-profit, or educational.

I discovered the generals who led U.S. troops through the four major conflicts of the latter half of the 20th century were human beings who demonstrated intangible strengths and worked through a series of their own vulnerabilities. Some people might reference their actions as wise, mindful, or emotionally intelligent. I found their stories inspirational. The basic lessons I took from the generals who led the four major conflicts can be summarized as: (1) Offer Second Chances, (2) Be Present, (3) Attune and Adapt, and (4) Enlarge Perspective. These leadership practices bring to mind the five EQ-i 2.0 emotional intelligence composites described in Chapter 2: self-awareness, self-expression, interpersonal, decision-making, and stress management. Figure 9.1 illustrates the parallel relationships between the EQ-i 2.0 composites and the mindfulness exhibited by the generals who led the U.S. Armed Forces during World War II, the Korean conflict, the Vietnam War, and the first Gulf War. The following sections expand my reflections from Ricks' excellent history.

SECOND CHANCES

Offering second chances is the leadership lesson I pulled from Rick's coverage of World War II and General George C. Marshall. In today's 24×7, fast-paced business world, how many people do you know who received a

Self Awareness

Self Expression

Interpersonal

Decision Making

Stress Management

OFFER SECOND CHANCES

BE PRESENT

ATTUNE and ADAPT

ENLARGE PERSPECTIVE

Emotional Intelligence Composites

Military Leadership Success Parameters

FIGURE 9.1
Non-tangible leadership skill comparisons.[6]

second chance after making a mistake? Marshall was a believer in train-ing, education, and experience. Although he was known to remove inept officers from their command, there were instances during the war when Marshall realized that a previously high-performing general was becom-ing battle weary and initiated what some people refer to as Marshall's 4R policy: relief, reassignment, recharge, return.

My observation of second chances is based on the 4R policy which Marshall demonstrated by recognizing that an officer under his command was exhausted and needed relief from the stress. He pulled them from active combat command and reassigned them to oversee a training camp for a year or two. The generals were competent; they simply needed a break from the stress of front line combat. They were able to recharge and share their experience with the new recruits and rising officers. When they were ready, he brought them back to the battlefield where, in most instances, the returning general was very successful.

Marshall extended similar grace to the younger, less experienced soldiers. One of his signature programs was an "err and learn" policy that provided his staff a second chance to learn from a mistake. His program demonstrated the respect and trust he had for the people who reported to him.[7] Peter Dawkins, a West Point graduate, wrote an arti-cle for *Infantry* magazine in 1965 recalling the Marshall system and the military leadership framework it supported throughout the 1950s and early 1960s. He quoted the General, "… If [a man] is to pursue a bold and vigorous path rather than one of conformity and acquiescence, he will sometimes err."[8]

CONSIDER AND DELIBERATE

Describe a time when you made a mistake, corrected it, and took the lesson forward.

Create a timeline of the process described in the above question. Identify what you were feeling at each milestone (e.g. mistake identification, confession, asking for help, problem resolution, next steps)

How did your relationship with the people involve change? Or, did your relationships remain the same?

Describe a professional or personal situation where you were able to provide someone else a second chance.

Create a timeline of the process described. Identify what you were feeling at each milestone (e.g. problem identification, coaching, and problem resolution)

How did your relationship with this person change? Or, did it remain the same?

Strong bonds develop between people who have worked through tough challenges together. Even civilians can feel as if they are in the middle of a firefight when a deadline must be met and people realize the requirements changed, the budget didn't, and several unforeseen challenges arose. Working together with someone to conquer what appears to be insurmountable makes the journey just a bit easier.

BEING PRESENT

The importance of being present is the lesson I took from the Korean War. General Douglas MacArthur tried commanding troops during the Korean Conflict from Tokyo. This was not a successful strategy and there were many difficulties for the ground troops. General O.P. Smith who was the Marine commander in Korea and General Matthew Ridgeway who reported directly to General MacArthur took a more hands-on approach to rectify the poor troop morale, instill confidence, and improve combat leadership strategies.

Both Smith and Ridgeway believed in leadership by example. General Smith is credited with turning the tide of the Chosin Reservoir Campaign. Military historians attribute the success to his attention to details during the planning phase that preceded the attack. When he arrived in Korea, the troops were scattered across the geography. He consolidated the regiment so the Marines could provide better support for each other once the fighting started. The second essential part of Smith's plan was his order to build two air strips which enabled supplies to be flown in and wounded soldiers to be moved out quickly. Lastly, Smith positioned himself at a location that he determined would be a key point during the battle. By being physically present, he would be able to make immediate and knowledgeable decisions.

General Ridgeway believed a combat commander needed to be near the zone of action and that a person could not lead others without an established connection. Humility and diplomacy were two of his most admired traits. He was very aware of the need to balance what he felt needed to be done while handling General MacArthur, to whom he reported, very carefully. His first action when he arrived in Korea was to visit the South Korean president to assure him the Americans were going to stay to help the South Koreans fight. He then visited the battlefield commanders to assess their readiness and morale. Next on his agenda was visiting with as many enlisted soldiers as possible to reinforce his promise, "You will have my utmost. I shall expect yours."[9]

The attention Generals Smith and Ridgeway placed on their most important resource—the soldier—is a tremendous lesson to take forward. Being present to recognize and provide for the day-to-day needs of the people who perform the organization mission creates a solid foundation of trust and confidence to follow leaders as they maneuver forward during times of change and uncertainty.

CONSIDER AND DELIBERATE

Describe a time when you worked for a manager who "phoned it in." How did it affect the quality of your effort and that of your colleagues?

Describe a time when someone you respected asked you to put in some extra hours in order to achieve a goal. How did you feel when the request was made?

If you put in the extra time requested, how did you feel while doing the work? How did you feel when the task was complete?

Being present involves two-way communication. Often no words are exchanged; however, the weight of the moment is not placed on a single person's shoulders. The exchange that happens when leaders are "present" lightens the load from the task owner's shoulders because they know they are not bearing the responsibility alone.

ATTUNE AND ADAPT

The need to adjust strategies to meet the needs of the current situation is the basis for the "Attune and Adapt" lesson that I pulled from the Vietnam War. The early relationships between the U.S. military and the South Vietnamese were very difficult after the French military left Vietnam in the 1950s. There were some very difficult communication challenges. The early U.S. military leadership essentially ignored any discussions with the French transition team or the South Vietnamese. They were confident the same tactics the U.S. military used to win World War II could be deployed with a successful outcome in Vietnam.

With each change of U.S. military leadership, the World War II strategies and methods which proved successful in the open battlefields of Europe continued to be deployed. Even when General William Westmoreland and General William DePuy took their commands leading the Vietnamese campaign during the mid-1960s, they would not consider that an alternate strategy could be more effective. Robert Komer, a CIA officer assigned to the Vietnam pacification program in 1967, described the situation as,"... rather than shift to what it needed to do, the Army would continue doing what it knew how to do. ... We went and fought the Vietnam War as if we were fighting the Russians in the plains of central Europe for a very simple, straight-forward reason—that was what we were trained, equipped, and configured to do." [10]

General Creighton Abrams, Jr. replaced General William Westmoreland in mid-1968. After consulting with a variety of stakeholders and initiating two-way discussions, he shifted the overall strategy to focus on pacification programs that emphasized protection of the villages and the Vietnamese people. He implemented a three-layer approach the Marines had successfully deployed in remote areas. This strategy used large forces where necessary, but deployed smaller guerilla-type patrols in the areas around population centers and deployed infantrymen in the villages to protect and build trust among the villagers. This new strategy surprised the Viet Cong who were not able to respond quickly and suffered significant setbacks. [11]

The Vietnam War continues to hold a difficult place in American military history; however, the lessons to attune and adapt demonstrated by Abrams are invaluable at any time. A strategy that is successful within one environment will not necessarily work in another environment. Time, budget, resources, skill sets, and culture need to be considered as leaders select the best path to take. Making time to listen to stakeholder feedback and having the courage to view the situation from a variety of perspectives are basic tools that every leader should keep within easy reach.

CONSIDER AND DELIBERATE

Describe a time when you were involved in a situation where each person had a different view of what success looked like. Was the team successful or did they disband?

How did people handle their frustration?

How could the situation have been handled differently?

Once people find a comfort zone that has been successful, it can be very difficult to explore any other means to accomplish a similar task. Their expertise and strengths were hard won, so why should they try a different way that might not be successful? Brand loyalty is a great example of this phenomenon. Do you continue to use a cleaning product because that is what your mother used? Are you hesitant to try a new food or a spice because it is different from what you are used to eating? It takes courage and tenacity to look for situational differences and alternate methods.

ENLARGE PERSPECTIVE

Looking at a situation through multiple lenses to enlarge your perspective is the lesson I pulled from the first Gulf War. General Colin Powell and General Norman Schwarzkopf served as young officers in Vietnam where they learned the importance of becoming attuned to different circumstances and adjusting behaviors accordingly. In their effort not to repeat the mistakes made during the Vietnam War, they focused on coalition building and worked to involve stakeholders from different organizations and countries as they developed and adapted strategies appropriate for the Middle East.

One of the primary differences between the Vietnam and Gulf Wars is the diversity of cultures. From a cultural perspective, there were many similarities between the South and North Vietnamese peoples. Few, if any, of the allied and combatant countries involved with the Gulf War conflict shared a common culture, religion, or tribal affiliation. Both General Powell and General Schwarzkopf's success are attributed to their ability to look at a situation through the lenses of each stakeholder before deploying military action. There were few unforeseen consequences. If a mishap occurred, strong relationships had been built so that the appropriate leaders worked through whatever challenging issues arose. These collaborative actions are considered very positive demonstrations of modern leadership.

The network-centric technologies that were developing throughout the 1990s added another layer to complexity for combat zone decision-making. Schwarzkopf had to be careful not to allow his focus to become too narrow as he analyzed the large amounts of available data to him. If he allowed himself to deep dive into the vast amount of information, he might miss the forest for the trees. He also needed to view the data through several different lenses to assure his final decision considered the potential consequences from logistical, socio-cultural, and political perspectives.[12]

CONSIDER AND DELIBERATE

Reflect on a time when you had decided on a particular course of action, but made changes because of new information which had not been available earlier. Briefly describe the initial activity.

How did you receive the significant information which caused the change of plan? Was it discovered as part of a correction? Or did it come from a source which was not included during the initial planning process?

What type of change process did you work through to incorporate the new information into the established design/plan? How confident did you feel when you made the decision to shift from the original plan?

With the benefit of hindsight was there anything you could have done during the initial planning phase to have discovered the information sooner and incorporated it into the original plan?

Coalition building and stakeholder engagement are essential first steps for leaders who are venturing into new endeavors that will require innovative thinking. Bringing a variety of perspectives together will help you to broaden your perspective and practice empathy as you work to fully understand the consequences which might affect another group of people. Working with a coalition of stakeholders also will help you to identify and mitigate situations that could possibly prevent the success of your mission/project. Coalition members also can help you to build relationships with people who might not respond positively to you without a stakeholder's friendly intervention.

LEADERS AND LEARNING

The leadership lessons modeled by the generals who led the U.S. Armed forces are summarized within Table 9.3. Although the four themes are action-oriented, the generals who demonstrated these

TABLE 9.3

Mindful Military Leadership Lessons

Major Conflict	Leadership Lessons Learned
World War II	Offer Second Chances
The Korean Conflict	Be Present
The Vietnam War	Attune and Adapt
The First Gulf War	Enlarge Perspectives

traits pursued these actions as part of a continuous reflective learning/ planning cycle.

The continuous learning cycle begins as a defined undertaking with a focus on assuring the actions align with the organizational values. The second part of this learning/planning cycle involves the process of eliminating as many known challenges before they happen. Once the execution of the plan begins, leaders must help to mediate the consequences from unexpected risks as they happen and flexibly adapt as the changes require.

Leaders often are described as people who are curious and interested in different ideas and new perspectives. With so many workplace demands that require leaders to constantly seek information, analyze risks, and execute outcomes, how do they have the energy to pursue additional areas of knowledge? The answer is the energy they expend exploring new ideas is actually an investment in their personal development. Learning is an intrinsic means for leaders to maintain a broad perspective of the greater environment. In addition to honing a leader's competitive expertise; learning is a way to take a break from the details and responsibilities of day-to-day decision-making and enable people to see beyond the proverbial weeds.

OVERLAYING LEADERSHIP MODELS

Coming full circle back to the Diamond Leadership Model described in Chapter 1, Figure 9.2 overlays the four leadership lessons demonstrated by the 20th-century generals on top of the intangible facets of trust, confidence, humility, integrity, and empathy. When General Marshall offered a second chance to a rising officer, he demonstrated self-confidence that enabled him to tell a direct report that he was confident in his abilities and provided them opportunities to succeed.

FIGURE 9.2
The diamond leadership model with military leadership overlay.

General Smith and General Ridgeway demonstrated integrity when they situated their command posts in close proximity to the troops. Being present and paying attention to the day-to-day operational needs reinforced their commitment to their reporting officers and troops that they would be there to support them for the duration.

General Abrams demonstrated humility as he recognized the unique qualities of Vietnamese culture and geography and the necessity for the U.S. military to realign and adapt long-held strategies.

General Powell and General Schwarzkopf demonstrated empathy as they looked at the Gulf War challenges through multiple lenses to consider how the ensuing consequences would affect each stakeholder group.

TAKING LEADERSHIP LESSONS FORWARD

Personal growth is an essential element of the reflective learning/planning cycle. Referring back to the Organizational Clarity Model discussed in Chapter 3 (Figure 9.3), leaders work to balance the relationships among organizations and working groups.

Even without the impetus of a significant change, leaders should continue to reflect and verify that the balance among their organizations and associated working groups continue.

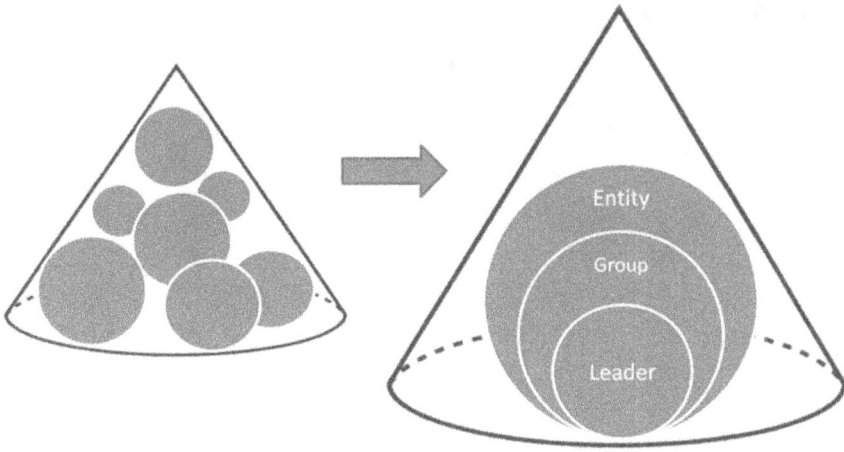

FIGURE 9.3
Organizational clarity model.

A BALANCED LEADER

Neil Pasricha, author of *The Happiness Equation,* wrote an article for *The Toronto Star* about why people should never retire. As part of his discussion, he referenced the fact that there is no Japanese word for retirement. This led to him discussing the term, Ikigai, which roughly translates "the reason you get out of bed in the morning."[13] Ikigai is an ancient Japanese thought process that helps people to determine their life purpose. It is based on four crucial questions that are meant to help a person realize how they can contribute to the world around them.

Figure 9.4 illustrates the interconnections of the Ikigai concepts which balance an individual's passion, mission, profession, and vocation.[14] To discover your Ikigai, ask yourself four questions.

1. What do I love?
2. What are my talents?
3. What can I do to earn money from my talents?
4. What does the world (or someone) need?

Do not write down the first answer that pops into your head. Take your time and reflect on your values and inspiration. How do the answers to the

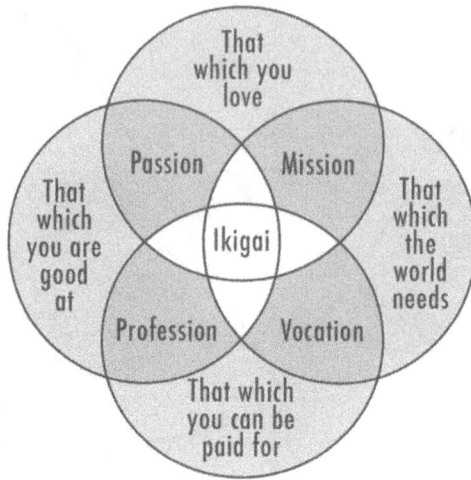

FIGURE 9.4
Ikigai life-balance model.

four questions interconnect with your current reality and what you want to be in your future?

As you work through this exercise to identify your passion and personal goals, remember this is a fluid process that may take several iterations. Your answers will change. As your environment and worldview change, your passions and personal goals may change as well. What was once extremely urgent to you may no longer be even a small priority.

Pasricha cited a comprehensive study of 43,000 Japanese adults in his article for the *Toronto Star*. This study discovered people who practiced Ikigai were happier, healthier, and had lower levels of stress than those who did not pursue this self-reflective practice. Pasricha's basic message is that finding an activity or cause that makes you feel purposeful and happy will help you maintain constructive connections with your surrounding environment. This applies to both your workplace and other personal pursuits. He recommends the long-proven Ikigai method as a means to help you find your personal north star aka your personal reason for being.[15]

Some people are able to wholeheartedly pursue their passion as their life mission. The Ikigai principles identify these people as being able to delight in life's fullness, but they will have no wealth. On the opposite end of the spectrum, people who place all of their emphasis on their professional vocations may have great wealth, but will most likely maintain a nagging sense of emptiness. People who focus their energies on honing their talents will feel useful, but may not take part within the greater society. Lastly, people who focus specifically on what the world needs will feel short term excitement about their effort toward achieving the mission; however, they may have a sense of uncertainty regarding their longer term path.

It is a very fortunate person who can lead a life in which these four elements intersect.[16] This intersection often is referenced as a point of joy. So the truly big conundrum to work through is the answer to the question, what brings you joy?

CONSIDER AND DELIBERATE

Given a single day without any responsibilities or places to be (yes, the children are with a trusted caregiver) what would you do?

Given one week with the same freedoms as the question above, and an unlimited budget, what would you do?

Who is the one person you have met within your lifetime, even briefly, with whom you would like to spend an uninterrupted afternoon talking? Why?

Select the 3–5 people you consider closest to you (friends, family, or colleagues). What one gift do they share with you? And, what is the one gift you share with each of them?

Everyone has their own definition of joy. Sometimes we get so busy with the work-a-day world and making sure the people who work with us are successful, we forget to prioritize our own personal development. Emotionally Intelligent leaders take a few minutes each day to reflect on their priorities, goals, and what is bringing them joy. Ikigai is one way for you to focus on your professional and personal desires and what is required to achieve them. These private reflective moments may enable you to uncover thoughts and possibilities that lurk in the recesses of your brain waiting for the time, place, and opportunity to be revealed.

As this final chapter concludes, please remember the following hard-learned lessons:

- Practice kindness to yourself and others
- Be generous with your attentions
- Be direct in your conversations—say what needs to be said
- Different situations will require different leadership skills/strengths
- Mistakes happen—forgive yourself and others
- Acknowledge failure as a learning opportunity
- Offer second chances, Be present, Attune and Adapt, Enlarge your perspective
- Continue to seek out your passion

NOTES

1 Rovelli, Carlo. (2017). Reality Is Not What It Seems: The Journey to Quantum Gravity. New York, NY: Riverhead Books. Translated by Simon Carnell and Erica Segre.

2 Tippett, Krista. On Being. (March 16, 2017). "All Reality is Interaction."

3 Keltner, Dacher. (October 2016). "Managing Yourself Don't Let Power Corrupt You." *Harvard Business Review.* pp. 112–115

4 Ludeman, Kate and Erlandson, Eddie. (Fall 2016). "Coaching the Alpha Male." How to Work with Toxic Colleagues. *Harvard Business Review On Point.* pp. 62–72

5 Ardi, Dana, PhD. (2013). *The Fall of the Alphas: The New Beta Way to Connect, Collaborate, Influence—And Lead.* (pp. 188–191). New York, NY: St. Martin's Press.

6 ©2017 by Susan Schwartz of the River Birch Group. Reprinted with permission.

7 Ricks, Thomas. (2012). *The Generals: American Military Command from World War II to Today.* (pp. 24–39; p. 451). New York, NY: The Penguin Press.

8 Ricks, Thomas. (2012). *The Generals: American Military Command from World War II to Today.* (p. 213). New York, NY: The Penguin Press.

9 Ricks, Thomas. (2012). *The Generals: American Military Command from World War II to Today.* (pp. 150–181). New York, NY: The Penguin Press.

10 Ricks, Thomas. (2012). *The Generals: American Military Command from World War II to Today.* (pp. 217–264). New York, NY: The Penguin Press.

11 Ricks, Thomas. (2012). *The Generals: American Military Command from World War II to Today.* (pp. 315–326). New York, NY: The Penguin Press.

12 Ricks, Thomas. (2012). *The Generals: American Military Command from World War II to Today.* (pp. 367–394). New York, NY: The Penguin Press.

13 Pasricha, Eric. (2016). *Why North Americans Should Consider Dumping Age-Old* Retirement. The Star.com. Retrieved April 24, 2017 from https://www.thestar.com/life/relationships/2016/09/06/why-north-americans-should-consider-dumping-age-old-retirement-pasricha.html

14 Winn, Marc. (May 14, 2014). What is your Ikigai? Retrieved May 1, 2016 from http://theviewinside.me/what-is-your-ikigai/

15 Pasricha, Eric. (2016). *Why North Americans Should Consider Dumping Age-Old* Retirement. The Star.com. Retrieved April 24, 2017 from https://www.thestar.com/life/relationships/2016/09/06/why-north-americans-should-consider-dumping-age-old-retirement-pasricha.html

16 (dreamtime.com), Pasricha, Eric. (2016). *Why North Americans Should Consider Dumping Age-Old* Retirement. The Star.com. Retrieved April 24, 2017 from https://www.thestar.com/life/relationships/2016/09/06/why-north-americans-should-consider-dumping-age-old-retirement-pasricha.html

CHAPTER SUMMARY

Leaders Are Human Too

- Leadership is not about a single person or group. It is about the interconnections between organizational systems and the relationships that connect people to make success happen.
- A power paradox is a phenomenon that appears when an executive who has risen through the ranks practicing collaborative

leadership traits begins to demonstrate behaviors based on their newly acquired rank which could be described as selfish and unethical.

- Leaders often are divided into categories based on their personalities and associated behaviors. Alpha-type leaders tend to be very ambitious, competitive, and lead from a top-down approach. Beta-type leaders tend to be less aggressive and encourage collaborative workstyles. Neither type is good or bad. Each can be more effective in different environments.

- The Military Leadership Success model is based on four parameters pulled from each of the four major conflicts of the 20th century. These four parameters are: offer second chances, be present, attune and adapt, and enlarge your perspective.

- The most effective leaders are those people who never stop learning. Ikigai is an ancient Japanese process that offers people a structured methodology that can be applied to both your workplace and personal pursuits to help you determine the direction of your learning efforts.

Index

Note: Locators in *italics* represent figures and **bold** indicate tables in the text.

For Product Safety Concerns and Information please contact our EU
representative GPSR@taylorandfrancis.com
Taylor & Francis Verlag GmbH, Kaufingerstraße 24, 80331 München, Germany

www.ingramcontent.com/pod-product-compliance
Lightning Source LLC
Chambersburg PA
CBHW061210220326
41599CB00025B/4593

9 781032 859705